Cabot Tower, Bristol

Cabot Tower, Bristol: erected in 1897 to mark the 400th anniversary of a famous journey across the seas. John Cabot, an Italian navigator, was commissioned by an English king to find a new sea-passage to the Far East. Instead, he and his Bristolian crew were the first known Europeans to 'discover' the North American continent.

Contents

NatWest Life is pleased to have been associated with South West Arts in the production of previous books in this series of writings by Bristolians. By encouraging new authors to write about their experiences in their own words, this series has tapped into a rich vein of talent and brought pleasure to many.

We are particularly pleased to be sponsoring the publication of 'Origins', which addresses the roots from which so many in this multi-ethnic city come.

I have the honour of chairing the South West region's Race for Opportunity campaign, which encourages companies to get closer to their ethnic minority customers and suppliers. Through this, I have become very much aware of the enthusiasm of so many in the communities for their adopted city, despite some of the problems they -- or their families before them -- have faced. These themes -- and many others -- are well reflected in the accounts in this book.

NatWest Life adopted Bristol as its home when we opened for business here in January 1993. We have been welcomed here and our support for 'Origins' reflects a desire to continue to play our part in our local community.

I wish future success to all the writers included here -- in the field of writing and elsewhere.

GERALDINE EDWARDS
'Origins' Project Co-ordinator

About the Project

'Origins' is the result of a two-year community publishing project co-ordinated by the Bristol Literature Develop-ment Project. The stories were produced through, firstly, writing workshops led by Bertel Martin, a Bristol poet of Jamaican heritage and Anjum Malik, originally from Pakistan, now a resident of Manchester, who writes poetry in both Urdu and English; and secondly, through recorded interviews and smaller workshops led by Jamila Yousaf, writer and broadcaster, and myself.

It came about because I had spent two years in Asia and had been fascinated by the way whole communities of one part of the continent left their homes, 'upped sticks' and settled thousands of miles away, creating another community in a far away city. Not just creating another separate community, but adding another layer of culture, language, music, philosophy (and monetary wealth) which made that particular city unique. The Chinese, just one example, have left the mainland and made their homes, not just in Singapore, Taiwan and Hong Kong, but all over Asia -- Malaysia, Indonesia, Vietnam and Thailand. The same is true of nationals of every country in the world. When I came back to England I felt that so many of us living here are 'immigrants' or children of immigrants, yet so much energy is used up in the desperate need to assimilate or blend into the background, that the personal epic tale of the journey to England becomes hidden inside every individual. I am convinced that people who travel thousands of miles to find a home, leaving their roots, usually for ever, bring a special vitality to the city, town or village that receives them. Migration, for whatever reason, be it a question of survival or a fulfilment of a dream, is remarkable -- and has been going on for thousands of years.

My heartfelt thanks go to all the contributors who participated enthusiastically and bravely, exposing their experiences here, in most cases for the first time.

Acknowledgements

I would like to thank the following individuals and organisations for their support, work and advice on the project:

The workshop writers Bertel Martin and Anjum Malik, Jamila Yousaf (workshop writer and translator), photographers Nina Belluomo, Sabera Bham and Carlos Laprida, teachers Pabitra Ghosh and Alison Fry from St Georges Community School, the Barbados and Caribbean Friends Association, the Sikh Resource Centre, the Barton Hill Asian Women's Resource Group, Davar, the Jewish Institute in Bristol, the Polish community of Bristol, the Bristol Vietnamese Refugee Community, Marian Liebmann, Christina Malkowska Zaba, Black Pyramid Films, Anne Malindine, John Sansom and the Redcliffe Press, and other members of the Management Committee -- Sara Davies, David Onamade, Malcolm Reed, Patrick Ismond and Julie Williams -- and Les Blythe from NatWest Life.

Photographers are credited against their work, except for front cover (Nina Belluomo) and rear cover, bottom (Sabera Bham).

Across the Seven Seas

It was in 431 BC that the Greek playwright Euripides wrote: 'There is no sorrow above the loss of a homeland.' I suspect there is. When life forces you to leave your birthplace, there is forever a sore spot in your heart. But if the place you end up living and possibly dying in turns out, in many cases, to offer you refuge without love the sore is chafed again and again, making healing impossible. That anguish is much worse than the original suffering of exile whether imposed or self-imposed. Other feelings also arise which are barely understood by those who have never had such experiences.

For many immigrants there are myths which die hard and others for whom hope of return has to be surrendered. If yours was a decision forced upon you by circumstance, there is so much unfinished business you carry with you. Your country of origin changes beyond anything you can imagine and still you cling to the images you carried with you, like tea in a thermos flask which slowly goes cold and loses its flavour. Your children are born in this country thinking they will be embraced the way you couldn't be because you were from over there and they are of this soil. They learn that only a small part of these expectations will be met. They don't understand your ways (how can you expect them to?) and you know, as an immigrant parent, that this is only the first step to the long road which will take them away from you, leading to the loss of long ancestral connections.

Meanwhile as you become part of the first world, you have to live with the fact that poorer countries continue to suffer while (if you are lucky and can work and have worked three times as hard as the indigenous people) you have your carpets and tiled bathrooms. The relationship with the country you emigrated to remains a complicated one. Do you always appear grateful? Do you have the right to criticise the country which gave you your shiny bathroom or can you only allow yourself to do this in the privacy of your own language behind closed doors? And what about your own people? As a member of the minority community are you ever free to say what you wish about them or are you bound in some tacit bond which forces you to protect their good name and which denies you freedoms to speak, however gently, however lovingly?

All these thoughts rose in my head as I read this wonderful collection of words by individual immigrants who broke through the awful barriers of being seen only as numbers and who were able to portray in such a live and moving way their lives, thoughts and dreams and how the past and future dovetail.

A couple of years ago I wrote my autobiography about my life as an Asian girl, then woman, living in Uganda, in a family which had neither money nor that emotional constancy which can sustain you through the most deprived times. My mother was a heroine. She kept us together and kept us laughing, working until it nearly killed her when my father disappeared as he frequently did. I had felt the need to do this for years but fear had kept me from trying. I knew I had to write fact not fiction in this book, though looking back I realise fiction might have been safer and more sensible. My father was a clever man but a failure as a father and a husband. When I was born all the rooms in his heart seemed to be occupied or locked up. I had a brother I loved who turned harsh as I became a teenager and a sister who was sent to this country when she was much too young. For years she was written out of our lives. I was lucky. Before I went mad -- for I was a melodramatic child -- I met my ex-husband and his large, warm yet squabbling, poor yet bonded and best of all normal family. I fell on them with happiness and gratitude and for two decades their love and faith sustained me.

Then I came to this country in 1972, when Asians were expelled from Uganda by Idi Amin. Dis-possessed of a country now I found myself in a land which I both loved too much in my dreams and feared too much in my waking hours. Neither prepared me for the horror of the racism that greeted us and followed us for years. Nothing can prepare you for this, and from a people who were meant to be the most civilized in the world.

Then my husband of that time suddenly left me for a young blonde student. I had a ten-year old son. The past betrayals came back to haunt every corner of my life. I had such grief -- for the lost love of a father, brother and now husband -- that writing the book seemed the only way to cope. It was one way, too, of keeping our history, our narratives from dying. The book was also trying to grapple with other dark and difficult issues. As Asians in Uganda, we had occupied the middle zone between whites and blacks. We had grown arrogant and prejudiced. Our ancestors who had come before us as explorers and traders treated blacks with respect. Time and money had fattened us and spoilt us. I felt guilt, as people spoke about Uganda as if it was full of tyrants and we its pitiful victims. This was part of the truth and we had been treated appallingly by the black leadership. But most black Ugandans I had known were even more grossly betrayed by their rulers. Three quarters of a million of them were killed. Surely it was

wrong for us Asians not to see what mistakes we had made or even consider what had happened to black lives in that same period?

The book was written and hell came for a long while to stay. So many taboos had been broken. An Asian woman does not tell the terrible secrets of her family life. She rarely tells the good tales either. My brother refused to speak to me ever again. My community thought I was mad, bad and dangerous. White people, some my friends, were alarmed by my descriptions of white racism. My pride in writing this book which was hailed by all the newspaper critics in this country gathered dust. Then, bit by bit, things changed. People in my community have begun to read it with an open mind and some say they love what I wrote. This is the power of the written word.

The words in this book, too, will annoy some and create reactions never anticipated. But in time something else will happen. The children of immigrants and the rest of the country will understand how much we have brought to this country and how much it has cost each of us. They will also see how strong, talented and brave you have to be to do what the people featured here have done. And that it is all around Bristol, that city which is still a powerful reminder of some of the more ignoble parts of British history, will make it all the more powerful.

Yasmin Alibhai-Brown is a journalist and writer and also a Research Fellow at the Institute for Policy Research. She is the author of "No Place Like Home", which explores the issues around displacement and is currently writing a book about Feminism and Black and Asian women, to be published by Penguin Books.

Last Train from Hell

In the summer of 1939 at the age of sixteen I was in the second year at the Technical Training Institute, 'ORT', in Berlin. The official name of our school was: Joint British Committee ORT-OZE.

It was not the least the name which pointed to British ownership of the school, which a year earlier had protected us from severe persecution on the night of the pogrom in November 1938. It had been said for some months that part of the school and its teaching staff were to emigrate to Leeds in England. Up until then the emigration date had been postponed repeatedly. The reason given was that both home and school in Leeds were not yet ready. We also had to wait for the German authorities to grant an export permit for the machines and tools belonging to the school.

At one point, when no particular intelligence could be found to indicate that war was imminent, the German school principals decided not to wait any longer for buildings to be made ready or for the machinery export licence to be granted, but rather to send the 100 pupils, who already had an entry from the British authorities, on their way as quickly as possible.

So two days before the outbreak of war we found ourselves travelling without personal luggage or money on one of the last trains still going from Berlin in the direction of the Dutch border.

Men, women and children were packed in tightly; they had been expelled from Germany partly because of their Polish, Jewish origins. There were also people who, like us young people, wanted to leave Hitler's Germany before the outbreak of the war which threatened us all.

The train travelled through the night and through my home town of Bielefeld, where my family was living, ignorant of the fact that I was on my way to a new home. Shortly before reaching the German/Dutch border Nazi customs officers boarded the train and demanded that we hand over our Jewish identity cards which only shortly beforehand, with the Jewish first name, Israel, we had had to get from the German police authorities.

One of the officers declared at the top of his voice, 'Now two very different parties are happy: we, to be rid of you and you, to be getting out of Germany.' How right he was. However, concern about the family of which by the end of the war, 28 had lost their lives in Riga and Auschwitz, did not allow any real rejoicing as we crossed the border.

From Holland we went by ship to England. From the Kitchener Camp in Richborough, Kent, I went to Leeds, Bradford and London. Following a short internment on the Isle of Man I volunteered for service with the British Army so as to take an active part in the fight against Hitler's Germany.

This is how I came to be in Germany once more, but this time in quite different circumstances. At the end of my military career I married my Rumanian wife in Germany. She had had to flee her country as a refugee from Stalinism. So I remained in the Federal Republic of Germany for the next 50 years.

One of my two sons settled in Bristol a few years ago as a doctor. I came to join him three months ago at the age of 74 to spend my old age among his family.

I shall never forget that it was Britain which saved me from destruction.

Synagogue, Park Row, Bristol

Helmut Gruenewald was born in Bielefeld, Germany in 1923 and emigrated to England in 1939. He became a voluntary member of the British Forces from 1944 to 1947 and was awarded a War Service Medal 1939-45. He was demobilised in Berlin in 1947 and resettled in Israel in 1948 until 1954. In 1957 he married Eritia Lessner who came from Czernowitz in Rumania. She died in 1986. Helmut served in the Israeli army and after release returned to Germany. After many years of working in business in Europe, writing several papers on Personnel and studying Psychology in Zurich, he settled in retirement in Bristol with his son, Dr Peter Gruenewald and his family. He now has two grandchildren in Bristol, and enjoys reading, writing, modern art, antiques and cooking.

Has this Suffering any Meaning?

Christmas 1940

Ranek, bylo jeszcze ciemno, mroz scinal krew w zylach.
Nam do pracy isc, kazano, jak zawsze, co dnia.
Slabym ciezko w sniegu brnac o wlasnych silach,
Czy i to cierpienie znaczenie swoje ma?

It was morning, yet dark, and frost froze blood in the veins.
We were ordered to work, as always, every day.
The weak struggled painfully through the snow,
Has this suffering any meaning?

Last year the Polish community in Bristol celebrated the 50th anniversary of their settling here. In 1947 Polish soldiers arrived; they were demobilised and gradually introduced to civilian life and the hard work they had been offered.

The question was asked: Polish soldiers, why are they here and what for? They were even told, 'the war is over, why don't you go back to Poland?'

Let me tell you briefly the story of their tragic past. On September lst, 1939 Germany invaded Poland. Hitler didn't do it alone. An agreement between Germany and Russia had been signed in August by Ribentrop and Molotov. Hitler expected Russia to invade Poland the same day, but Stalin had his own plans, to put it off for a later date. 'Let the Polish army become weak, then we enter.'

I remember that day vividly. It was Sunday, and I went with my friend to church, 12 kilometres from home. My intention was to pray for the safety of my father who was in the army. As we were coming back, we met a boy from the village who told us that this morning, September 17th, the Red Army had crossed the Polish border. He heard it on the radio. I was frightened. Russia had hit us from the east like a knife in the back.

My father returned home in October. They were told to put down their arms and go to where they liked. In a couple of weeks he underwent a series of interrogations. The Red Army took our horse, then they placed the posts to mark the land they took away ... Even our well was not ours any more. Russian language was introduced into schools straight away, with Communist doctrine as the main subject.

Then came February 10th, 1940. They arrested and deported to Russia about one and a half million Polish people: whole families, old, young, babies, expectant mothers ... There was nobody to speak for us. They scattered us all over Russia to work in forests, building railways, coal mines, all sorts of mines, including gold in Kolyma, from where there was no return. Others were in prisons, including General Anders in the Lubianka in Moscow. They were tortured and interrogated.

About 15,000 officers and intellectuals -- the war prisoners -- were placed in Kozielsk, Starobielsk and Ostaszkow. About 400 survived. More than 4,000 were shot and buried in Katyn Forest, others in Miednoje, near Charcow, and in other places. The murderers were never brought before an international tribunal.

In our camps, which were situated deep in the forest between Vologda and Archangelsk, the camp commandant welcomed us with the words: 'you have been brought here to work. You have to obey orders. No group meetings. Tomorrow take you tools and you shall

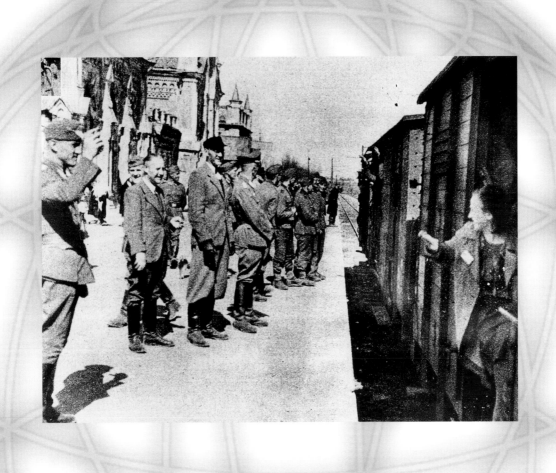

be taken to your place of work -- cutting trees. We can demand from you what we want, you cannot demand anything from us. Do not think that England or France will save you. You are here to work and die.'

We worked very hard, we were frost-bitten, struck by all sorts of illnesses, starving; some were interrogated, including my father, some were taken to prison. We were cut off completely from the outside world. There was no news that some of our soldiers had crossed the borders to Rumania, Hungary and Lithuania and had been interned. That Hitler was exterminating Jewish people and other peoples, including Poles. He established camps in Poland and Germany, aiming to exterminate all prisoners. They also captured young boys and girls to work on their farms. It was a real hell on earth.

We didn't hear about our airmen who had fled to Great Britain after Poland collapsed to take part in the Battle of Britain. Nor that some of our ships had sailed to British shores and fought the Germans on the seas.

In 1941, Germany broke its agreement and invaded Russia. One Polish woman -- a cleaner in the camp commandant's office -- had a young son. He was secretly sneaking into the office at night and listening to the radio. Then whispering secret news which circled the camp: 'the Germans have started war with Russia.' This built up our hopes for survival. Russia managed to deport yet more Poles to Siberia and Kazakhstan before Germany's advancing army.

On July 31st, 1941, General Wladyslaw Sikorski signed an agreement with Stalin to release all Polish prisoners and those in the camps -- so that they could join the Polish army in southern Russia to fight the Germans. We couldn't believe the news when, in early September, they gathered us in a club and announced the 'amnesty'.

We couldn't leave the camp yet as we had no transport. Some people walked to the station, about 80-100 kilometres away in deep snow and frost. We worked in the forest, cutting trees and roots to clear a way for a road; otherwise we couldn't buy bread and watery soup with little fish floating in it, or a slice of onion. More people were dying. I noticed my father's face starting to swell because of starvation. Suddenly, in February, a miracle happened. One of the civilian staff in the camp said, 'a tractor is going to the station tomorrow, and you may go with it'.

We were happy but at the same time afraid to make such a long journey. It took us two days and nights to get to the station and then -- would we find a train? We felt that God was protecting us, for a train was standing there the day we arrived. We travelled in cattle wagons for two long months, right from the north to the south of Russia in a starving country. Eventually we landed in Alma Ata near the Chinese border. In the meantime, General Wladyslaw Anders had negotiated with Stalin to let the army and civilians move to the Middle East. They were short of food and had no uniforms and no armoury. Dysentery and typhus were killers. Stalin agreed, and meanwhile the German army was heading for Moscow.

After a week in Alma Ata, our wagons were joined to an empty train and started off back towards the west. At Lugovaja, we were delighted to see our soldiers boarding the train, then we moved on. The train was now speeding, stopping only at the larger stations for a short time. I remember in Tashkent the fruit trees were covered with blossoms. Then, heading south, we arrived at the shore of the Caspian Sea. People were crying. Although weak and starving, we seemed somehow to find a little more strength to go through, checking our Russian documents, on to the wooden jetty where on one side was our ship; on the other, one for the troops. They packed us in like sardines.

In two or three days we were on the sands of Port Pachlevi in Persia [now Iran], another world, like paradise! We were free at last. Here we had our first open air Mass after two years. I wish there had been cameras to record it all.

It was Easter Sunday, 1942. Tents were put up by the English and Polish soldiers. Our food came from army kitchens.

After quarantine, we were moved to Teheran which is beautifully encircled by mountains. My father's health was improving; then we had sad moments, for he had to say goodbye and join the army. He left Teheran, went to Iraq, Palestine and Egypt, then sailing round the South African coast into the Atlantic and to Scotland to join the First Armoured Division under General Stanislaw Maczek.

My mother and I stayed in Teheran for about five months. Disease was killing people. We had to be careful what we ate as our stomachs were starved. In September, 1942 we were moved to the Persian Gulf and the ship City of London took us to Karachi. After a short rest, we sailed on the same ship across the Indian Ocean to Dar-es-Salaam in East Africa. For about 5½ years, women and children lived in the camps scattered over the African continent. We lost contact with my father for eighteen months.

At least we had peace and safety while our fathers, brothers and sons were fighting on all fronts hand-in-hand with the Western Powers. Their hope was to return to Poland and settle back in the area where they belonged in the east of the country. Others who had been captured by the Germans hoped to return to their homes in western Poland.

That hope was dashed, when on July 3rd, 1943 General Sikorski was killed in a plane crash in Gibraltar. Was it sabotage or an accident? He knew all the secrets of politics and how to negotiate with Stalin. Polish people everywhere were devastated.

On May 18th, 1944 the Polish 2nd Corps, which fought in Italy under General Anders, celebrated a great victory. They took over the monastery at Monte Cassino and on its rubble placed the white and red Polish flag. On August 4th, 1944, the Polish 1st Armoured Division under General Maczek started landing in Normandy to fight alongside the British and Canadian forces until the capitulation of Germany. General Anders wanted to join all the Polish forces in one and march into Poland to free our country from Russia so that we could all return home, but this failed.

On February 11th, 1945 the three great leaders -- Stalin, Churchill and Roosevelt -- met in Yalta near the Black Sea. The whole of eastern Poland was given to Russia. Poland became a Communist state as Stalin established a puppet government there and the leaders of the Polish army were Russians. In the west, Poland got Silesia from Germany, along with land up to the river Oder.

My father survived the war. He was with the British army on the Rhine. He wrote and asked what we should do. We had nowhere to go. Most of the soldiers decided not to go back under Communism. We agreed, but where should we go? There was no place like home.

In God's plans, there was a place for us, though. The British government granted political asylum to 140,000 Polish soldiers, promising to bring over their families in the near future. My father arrived in England in 1947 and worked in forestry near Taunton. My mother and I came on the ship Carnarvon Castle to Southampton in May 1948. We lived in the camp at Haydon near Sherborne for six years. I married, and our daughter was born. We worked very hard to save money for a deposit to buy our own home, after being homeless for fourteen years. In 1954, we bought our first house, delighted to have a roof over our heads. Then our second child, a son, was born in the Bristol Maternity Hospital.

Had this suffering had any meaning? It was worth all the effort and determination to survive, and the words spoken by a Russian soldier at the hour of our arrest -- 'do not cry, you are very young, your whole life is before you' -- came true.

Thank you, Bristol, for having us.

Stanislawa Cesarz was 14 when she and her family were deported to a Russian labour camp. After two years they were released and after an epic journey ended up in an African refugee camp, where she trained to be a nurse. Her father took part in the Normandy landings and at the end was part of the British Army of the Rhine. With her father already in England, Stanislawa arrived in 1948 and eventually settled in Bristol in 1954. She has written a book about her life, and is now a widow with two children and four grandsons. She belongs to a choir called 'Polish Flowers'.

Jewish families awaiting an uncertain fate

Black and White

I must have been about 23 when I came to England. I was working in Barbados with a company which matured and bottled rum. They also imported top class alcoholic products, such as whisky, but their main thing was to export rum, especially to Canada and the United States. I was their customs clerk, looking after import and export documents and overseeing the shipping.

The ships used to anchor in the bay offshore and you used to have to go on board to make sure the shipment was perfect, and had no breakages, because they used to take the product off by lighters and transfer them to the ship, and there were breakages.

Because you were working for a company which dealt with rum, they thought you were capable of drinking all day and all night! There had been one or two casualties with youngsters from other firms, and I thought this was getting a bit much, getting into the drink -- because I used to consider myself a bit of an athlete as well, and the two things didn't go together, and so that was one thing. But the most compelling thing was that I always wanted to be an engineer and I decided -- considering all things -- let's get on with this before I get too old. My brother was here in England, in Bristol, already established, I had written a few letters -- and I'm a terrible letter writer, by the way, it was quite a feat for me -- I suddenly decided to buy a ticket and go ...

One pre-conceived idea I had about coming to England was that I would spend three or four years becoming an engineer and that would be it, and I would go back to Barbados. But it was nearly seven years before I qualified and then one realised that there was very little production engineering in the West Indies, so there was no incentive as far as work was concerned.

Let me see what I thought about Britain at the time ... I knew there would be a lot more rain than we were used to, and that it would be continuous throughout the year. I thought the country would be more prosperous than it was. I thought the cities would be far cleaner. But Barbadians had a slightly different perception than other West Indians about whether white people worked or not -- I was brought up to know that quite a lot of Barbadians were poor white people. In fact, at one time at my aunt's farm there was a white cook. I did know there was a certain amount of poverty here, but I had no idea of its extent, so it was a bit of a surprise, rather than a shock.

Now one of the things that really shocked me was when I arrived in Liverpool. And perhaps what emphasised it more, was that the boat had come through Lisbon -- and Lisbon was absolutely beautiful, an absolutely beautiful city, and the reception area of the docks was wonderful -- like an airport reception with beautiful plants. But when we arrived in Liverpool, they must have had a shipment of cattle just before we docked and when we came off, the quay smelled to high heaven and you had to be careful where you stood -- it was covered in cow dung! It was disgraceful. We came down the gang-plank and just at the bottom was a cow pat -- you had to be careful not to step into it, there had been no attempt to clean up ... This was 1954.

I got a short distance away with my two bags and this steward came shouting down the gang-plank -- with this hat that I had left on board. In Barbados my mother had insisted that I buy one, an ordinary felt hat with a fairly broad brim because I was always working on the docks, and it helped keep the heat off the back of my neck. This was the thing I wore only when I was going on the docks, but when I was leaving Barbados, my mother insisted I took it with me because 'when you get to England you won't have the sun, it will be raining all the time, and you'll want to keep the water off your head, you can't go round with your hair full of water, dripping all the time. You take that hat with you!' There I was, at the bottom of the gang-plank, and the steward came and plonked it on my head, and I'd had to step back over this filth again.

We got through the customs and I had several hours to wait for the train to Bristol, so I thought I'd get a taxi driver to drive me around and show me Liverpool. We drove and drove and drove, and it was all this terrible drabness because at the time they hadn't cleaned up Liverpool after the war. I saw some dreadful looking places. I thought: 'if Bristol is anything like this, I'm on my way back!'

We got on the train and the countryside was lovely and green, so that was a relief. I thought it might not be so bad ... but coming into Bristol, it was pretty awful and even now it's not a very nice approach. Getting off the train, I left the hat on the top, I was about to step on to the platform, and this chap said, 'Sir, you've left your hat!' and I thought I was never going to get rid of it. The first thing my sister-in-law said when she saw me was 'get rid of that hat.' I said, 'I've been trying to ever since I left Barbados.' I should have thrown it overboard.

From the station, we drove to the Brislington area of Bristol where my brother lived, in Sturminster Road. There were quite a number of prefabs on a slightly low-lying area with the road raised from it. Most of the people there had been cultivating roses, and the whole valley seemed to be covered in beautiful colour. That was such a relief, and what's more the rose is my favourite flower! I grew up with my father cultivating roses, I grew up loving roses -- I still do -- and that made me feel very, very much better. From then on, for the next month or so, it rained

and rained and rained -- every day, I thought I would never see the sun again. I don't remember being cold, and the winters have never bothered me, I've always put on enough clothes. Even today, even in Britain, I have never felt as cold as I did once in a squall in Barbados.

It was seventeen years before I went back to Barbados. When I arrived in Bristol I stayed with my brother. I got a job with the company he worked for, Bristol Pneumatic Tools, and they gave me a sort of late apprenticeship in engineering, linked to what would become Brunel College, and in those days there was no day release for non-apprentices. We had to do our studying in the evenings and work at nights, and I had very little time other than going to work and going to college, for six or seven years. Nothing else.

I was never homesick. The only time I felt, not homesick, I suppose guilty, was first when my mother died, and then when my father died. I felt genuinely guilty for not being there and for having left. I have one sister still alive, but for many years I had two brothers still living there. And a sister who lived in St Lucia, and she died only last year. But I have really and truly quite enjoyed living here. I don't have any terrible tales to tell, I have never come up against anything.

But a conflict has arisen recently, since I retired. Muriel, my wife, has wanted to go and live in Barbados, but I don't want to. People might think it strange, but I have no great love of Barbados. To me it's just a nice place to go on holiday. What I have when I go there, rather than elation, is a bit of sadness. For what I knew of the place and my people's circumstances when I was a youngster, that's gone ... just a tenuous connnection ... it probably would be disappointing to go back and live there. You can escape it here, in Britain, but too many people in Barbados are too materialistic, and I would always be in serious conflict with people I considered to be my friends. I'm not prepared to get into that. I always was a socialist. My family were

reasonably well off. My father was a doctor. There were seven of us children, with me the last of the tribe. The first five of my brothers and sisters went to the best schools in Barbados and had a really spoilt childhood, I'm sure. I didn't quite get that treatment as my father went blind, and had to stop practising quite early in his working life, and things became less lucrative. I went to school and mixed with youngsters who were really poor and that has left a life-long impression on me.

I always wondered why even my family were not doing more to help these people. We lived in a fishing village. I don't like fishing, but I was always around the fishermen with their boats, and I knew what a tough life people had, so I was always a socialist at heart. I was a rebel in my family, and that has stayed with me always, very much reinforced in England -- when you see what life really is, and the fact I had no help with studying. The first exams I took had to be treated as part of my holidays, as we were not allowed time off. Even when I was doing my HNC, when I was working at Engineering Products at Clevedon, I wanted to take a week of my holidays so I could prepare for the examinations, but couldn't do so -- I had to take my holidays when the rest of the company took them. It toughened you up and you didn't ask for favours. You did what you had to do. And unfortunately too many people from the West Indies just caved in after a while. I'm sure a whole lot more could have done a lot better, advancing their education, if they'd had genuine encouragement. But no, they didn't.

Mrs Sealy: Don't forget, in the beginning we were colonials so we started the British Colonial Association. I was a founder member. The association was founded with the help of the Bristol Co-operative Society education department. They were a tremendous help. The Barbadians were always keen on education and progress, so they instilled in everyone that they must have a good education. And we had a welfare group, and we also had many more Jamaican than Barbadian members.

Most white people thought: 'they're all the same, they are all Jamaicans.' But it is pretty obvious that they come from different cultural backgrounds even if they are in the Caribbean. There are thousands of miles between Jamaica and Barbados. It was very difficult for the Barbadians, and eventually they became the West Indian Association, and then when we saw that things weren't going the way the Barbadians wanted, we split into West Indian Parents and Friends and Barbados and Caribbean Friends Association. In the beginning we were based in St Mary Redcliffe church hall. I believe the first meeting of the West Indian Association was in the White Hart pub here in St Paul's. We lived then in Sturminster Road, in Brislington. Most West Indians were in St Paul's or Eastville.

My first husband, Louis, came home one day and said, 'I've met a chap, a Barbadian, and there's quite a lot of them settled in Bristol. I've arrange to go to a meeting of these lads to see if we can start some kind of a social association.' They were meeting in pubs, and Louis came from a society where meeting in pubs was not that nice, especially for the wives. I went to the Coach and Horses in Braggs Lane, which was kept by a very old friend of mine, with her husband. She was shocked that I would go there, but I met all these people. It must have been about 1948, just after the war. Bristol didn't have many black families then.

We had a meeting in King Street with the British Commonwealth Association and it was they who suggested we call ourselves the Bristol Colonial Association. We used to have social nights and dances, it was really a social group. But we then realised that a few of the Jamaicans had come from middle-class families and were living in a way they didn't want to live, and that we should do some kind of welfare work, to see if we could

help them get out of the mire. We used to try to buy a house and get just two families living there.

When we became the Barbados and Caribbean Friends Association we still had a lot of our Jamaican and English members, and we went on with our welfare and education work, and still do today. We haven't really changed. Two of our members became JPs and two became city councillors.

Bill Smith, one of the JPs, and I used to go round the factories asking them to take on West Indian men and women -- women had to work then, they had no choice. I worked for three months for the Co-operative Society tailoring department to introduce girls on the production line -- I had never done it in my life, but I was willing to take three months out to do that. I worked on the line just to see what these girls were expected to do. I reckoned that if I could do it, they could do it, because I knew Barbadian women. The girls there used to say, 'Oh, you're married to a black man', and in those days if there was anything that used to annoy me intensely it was for people to talk about colour, because I don't believe in it. The only black person I know is an African, everybody else is of mixed race, so it doesn't make any difference. But they were so damned un-educated, they didn't even know where the West Indies were. And that used to annoy me. All they knew about was England, and maybe Ireland or Wales if they had some Welsh blood in them. They had such fantastic ideas about how people lived outside England. And they used to ask the most stupid questions, like did we have a table and chairs?

Television has done an awful lot of damage, but it's also done a lot to educate people on how others live. We in England would say, 'I'm going to make a stew', whereas the West Indians would say, 'I'm going to make a pot'. You couldn't get these native English people to understand that when the West Indians said they were going to do a pot, it was just a stew. The stupid things the English would say they thought would go in it! I wouldn't like to tell you! In those days the only rice the average English person had was rice pudding -- very few had rice with their vegetables. That kind of thing among the women used to make it awkward, you know.

I think the West Indian women did very well, dealing with the uneducated English. I cannot talk about the other islands, but the education standard in Barbados is very, very high. It didn't matter how poor you were, you were educated. Barbadian girls had to put up with an awful lot over here.

Now the younger generation have become world citizens. Most children of immigrants become world citizens. Although they say, 'I'm Jamaican', they don't really mean that. What they mean is they are of Jamaican extraction.

Mr Sealy: I've come to the conclusion that parents are largely responsible for some of the problems that these youngsters have, for the fact that many young people do not want to be seriously associated with what the older generation does. This is because the older people do not understand that their children are now British Black, they are not Barbadian, Jamaican, St Lucian or whatever. They are born in this country, educated here, they are British Black. They have an association with the West Indies but they are primarily British. Historically, it's a new, unique thing. These youngsters have grown up here, they don't know anything else.

Mrs Sealy: I can remember my grandson, John, saying once to a friend, 'I'm lucky, I've got a black grand-dad and I have a white grand-dad!', proud as can be, the fact that he had one of each.

BERTEL MARTIN

Grandmother

Chameleon on the limb
of the ackee tree
rock still tree brown
eyes absorbing everything
the stone veranda
wooden shops gravel garden
ancient grandmother
young grandson
reading to grandmother
in best english voice
grandmother says
how proud she is
of her grandson
who reads
in posh english

chameleon on the limb
of the ackee tree
absorbs all this
chameleon
not hiding

blending in
only the eyes show
it's a chameleon

now
walking all the city road
my grandmother's smile
is fading
but the chameleon
on the limb
blending in
still brings back
the heat and scent of Jamaica
my grandmother's home.

Bertel Martin is a Bristol poet who runs creative writing projects in schools and community groups. He also performs his work using elements of theatre, story-telling and cabaret.

Freedom

About a family who try to escape from a communist country, to gain freedom and happiness in another country.

1-- The Fall of the South of Vietnam

After South Vietnam fell in 1975, the Vietnamese communists took revenge on all the people of the south, especially those who were in the army or worked for the previous government. The communists took away all their possessions and jobs. They took whatever they could lay their hands on, and put the people in concentration camps.

Family after family suffered their loss, as they watched their years of hard work to earn a civilized life go down the drain. How they hated the communists!

My family happened to be one of these families. My father was in prison and my mother had lost her job as a teacher in a senior school. Nothing was going our way.

Shortly afterwards, I stopped going to school because I was unfairly and ill-treated by the communist teachers. I studied at home with the help of my mother, who was highly educated. We had great support from her family, which encouraged us a lot. My father's family were not in Vietnam at that time, and could not help.

Soon we were back on the right track, but we were still unhappy. We still did not have the freedom that we badly wanted. Having had a father who had a high rank in the army, which was considered a crime, was difficult, but we never stopped fighting for our freedom.

The communists continued punishing us, even though the war was over. My mother wanted us to start afresh in another country where I could grow up and have the freedom and education I had always longed for. So it was

decided. We would leave Vietnam. We knew the risks, but we just had to take them, no matter how it would end.

Three years on, when my father was finally let out of prison, we made arrangements to flee the country.

2 -- Take the chance

At that time, there was war between Vietnam and China. The communist government wanted to expel the Chinese and take over their properties and to prevent them from helping China spy on Vietnam. All the Chinese who had been living in Vietnam for many years were forced to leave by boat.

The Chinese, who were very good at business, knew that what many Vietnamese wanted more than anything was to leave Vietnam. They contacted the rich Vietnamese, especially those in the army or the professions, and told them they owned a boat and were leaving the country in a week's time. If anyone wanted to come, they must pay in gold immediately. In return, the Chinese would help the Vietnamese with false papers and disguise them as Chinese and, they hoped, get them aboard the boat.

It was not easy to escape from Vietnam. Not only the danger of being caught and imprisoned, but also being tricked by the dishonest Chinese and losing all the money that now took so long to earn. Some Vietnamese were unlucky to deal with Chinese 'con men', who took their money and were never seen again.

At that time, there were many tragedies. Many of the Vietnamese who had lost all their savings to the con men killed themselves and their families. Some lost their minds and died shortly afterwards.

Vietnam was dying and a new communist country was being born. The Vietnamese hated being ruled by the communists and having to obey their laws, but there was nothing to be done. More and more people wanted to leave.

My parents had made the hardest decision of their lives, to leave the country. They paid the required amount of gold to a boat owner and waited for further instructions. From then on, we lived under constant pressure. We didn't know if we could escape or whether we would end up like some of our unlucky countrymen who lost everything to the con men.

Every day that passed lessened our hopes. We could only pray. I still remember those endless, sad days when no one wanted to go out or do anything except wait for the Chinese men to come and take us away to the boat. The atmosphere was terrible, as it had been for seven months, with no message, no word, nothing. Finally, when we thought we were doomed, what we had waited for so long happened at last.

3 -- Escaping

It was a dark night. I was woken by my mother and given no time to ask questions but only told to get dressed quickly and quietly.

The day we had longed for had come, but my parents looked sad. I could see the tears in mum's eyes and still remember how sorrowful it was. She had to take that decision to leave the country, but deep down she didn't want to go. Who could blame her? No one can be happy when they are forced to leave their home country, leaving behind their dearest relatives. In order to go, we had to accept that we could never return.

In about ten minutes we were ready. We were disguised as Chinese and dressed in Chinese clothes. They were all so strange, I wanted to laugh but couldn't because of the look in my parents' eyes. We had a quick look around the house before leaving with the men. We were not allowed to bring anything except a small bag with a little food and water.

No one dared to make a noise as we walked quietly into the dark. People were sleeping and did not know what was happening. I wondered what they would say in the morning. I stopped thinking when I passed my grand-parents' home. My mother wanted to stop for a minute, but the Chinese men would not allow it. We walked to the waiting mini-bus about 100 metres away. When we arrived, we met another family already in the bus. We were then driven to another town about 100 kilometres away.

It was a quiet journey. We arrived at a quiet spot, to meet the boat owner and many other people. They were all Chinese, including the family we had met in the mini-bus.

4 -- Being alone

The Chinese seemed to be very excited about the journey. Vietnam was not their country, and meant nothing to them, especially as business was no longer good under the new communist government. But for the Vietnamese, leaving was painful.

The owner of the boat placed more strain on my parents by telling them that I should be left to go with a Chinese family so the police would not suspect that I or my parents were Vietnamese. They didn't want to do this, as I was so young, and wanted us all to be together at this dangerous time. But the owner insisted on separating us. He said he would bring us together again once we were safely aboard the boat.

My parents had no alternative but to accept. Mother explained everything to me briefly and begged me to go with the Chinese man and his family. I cried, and refused to leave my parents' side. Nothing was said as I was dragged away. My parents tried to put on a brave face but were desperately sad.

Two hours later, I was aboard the boat, after being checked thoroughly by the police. I stayed with the Chinese family until the boat was set off. It wasn't until an hour later that the boat began its long journey bound for Australia.

I was not reunited with my parents as the owner of the boat had promised, but as long as he had our money we had to depend on him. The Chinese family left me on my own while they went up on to the upper deck. I was left among total strangers, all Chinese. It was very frightening. The boat was so overcrowded that most of the people, me included, had to sit with their knees up against their chests. No one could move, because people were lined up all over the deck of the boat. This meant you could not move from one end of the boat to the other to get food.

The Chinese were very unpleasant to me, telling me to go away, but there was nowhere to go. I wanted to tell them I had as much right to be there as they had, but I was too afraid. Every night, I cried myself to sleep, thinking of my parents and my family in Vietnam to comfort me on this lonely journey.

5 -- Reunion

Eventually my dad found me. It was a great relief! I was so happy to be back in my father's arms, safe and sound. I was taken to another deck to meet up again with my mother. She was unwell, but we were back together again and that was our main concern.

Four days we had been aboard the boat with only a few oranges to keep us going. We knew that if we didn't find land soon we would die of starvation. There was no fussing or talking in the daytime. Everyone was too tired and weak to do anything but sit and mumble to themselves.

The chance of survival was slim. We had no food or water, but we did have ourselves and our family. As long as we were together we would always be happy, no matter how bad the situation was.

This journey had turned sour because of the communist government. They wanted the Chinese to die so they allowed only a limited amount of food aboard the boat. They knew this would last only a few days and not long enough for us to reach our destination.

It was not only the communists' fault. The boat owner had turned greedy and took over 500 people more than the limit of just 200 people. How could a boat only four metres wide and 20 metres long carry over 700 people? It was a miracle that everyone got on board. Most of the food and water were left behind, which made things even worse.

6 -- The dangerous time

We were coming to the fifth day of our journey, but were not sure we would live to see the day. The owner had told everyone that the boat was going to sink. There was too much strain and weight. It would hold out for only a few more hours. Everything heavy was thrown overboard, but still there was little hope of survival.

I can remember the reaction of some people when they heard the bad news. Some remained calm, but others panicked, screaming and crying hysterically. This wouldn't help anyone. We had a couple more precious hours to be together and we should use them wisely. I was glad that my parents stayed calm and faced the fact calmly. For the last remaining hours, we sat and prayed hoping that our prayers would be answered.

The boat quietened down after a while. Everyone now realised that they were wasting their energy by panicking while they could be with their families for the remaining time they had. The boat drifted on and on.

7 -- Rescued

Time was running out. We had only a few hours before the boat finally went down. The boat was quiet and still. All we could hear was the beating of the waves against the sides of the boat and the murmur of people praying. The minutes ticked by, and families huddled together.

'Look, look, a ship! A ship!' A man was shouting, pointing to the north. Everyone rose to their feet, looking anxiously. There it was. A ship. As it got nearer, we could just see the lettering on the side of the ship, 'The Sinbonga'.

It was a truly wonderful moment. Everyone was so happy, joking and laughing together. There were smiles all round, the first for a very long time.

Having seen our signal for help, the ship came nearer and nearer until it was anchored next to us. It was a cargo ship, carrying goods to Hong Kong. The captain knew at once of our dangerous situation and immediately ordered a rescue operation. Ropes were thrown over and tied to several parts of the boat. The able-bodied had to climb the ropes, while children and the elderly were hauled up in a kind of basket.

Fifteen minutes or so later, our boat went down. How lucky we were not to be going down with it. It was horrifying to watch. We had got to safety by the skin of our teeth.

The ship continued its course to Hong Kong. We were treated just like the crew, and there was kindness all round. There were several doctors aboard the boat. All those who were ill were treated until they were back on their feet.

8 -- In Hong Kong

When we reached land, we stayed in one of Hong Kong's camps, which was more like a prison, with high fencing around and soldiers everywhere. We had to share a room with 12 or 15 other people. We were badly fed and did not have regular washes, and still did not have the freedom we so badly wanted. We were forbidden to leave the camp in case we disappeared and did not return. Living there was as if we were back in Vietnam. We still did not have any freedom.

9 -- Arriving in England

After three long weeks at the camp, we moved on. We were taken by coach to an airport in Hong Kong, where we took a plane to England. Once in England we were taken to another camp called Sopley Reception Centre.

We settled down well. We were very happy there. I made many friends and at last had the freedom I wanted. I was taught to read and write and enjoy things that I had once enjoyed before Vietnam was taken over.

We had a little home of our own. It was really one big room, but it was something we could call our own. We stayed at the camp for six months and then we moved on. Our next destination was Bath.

10 -- A new life

Bath is miraculously beautiful. The people there are so kind and helpful. They helped us and encouraged us to continue when we were down and low, but now after seven years of hard work we have finally succeeded in life.

My dad is working in Bristol as the chairman of the Vietnamese Community. He is helping all those that are in need of help. I think it is wonderful. He has done so well that he has been congratulated by Prince Charles in person, and he has also received a medal from the Lord Mayor.

My mum has qualified as a technician, all in merits and distinction. She is working at the moment for an electrical firm in Bath. She has also been accepted to study at Bristol Polytechnic. If everything goes as planned next year she will take the engineering course there. She is very determined and I know that she will come top when she is finished.

I am a third year student at Ralph Allen School and doing well. I have everything that I have ever wanted and dreamed of. I just wish that all the unfortunate people in Vietnam will one day have the freedom and happiness that I have here in England.

[Written some years ago, while a third-year student at secondary school in Bath]

CHARLOTTE PEPLOE

From Vienna, 1938, We Send our Love

They came on the wheels of the train
pounding along the continent,
walking the waves, grinning with ignorance and
welcomed by some coastal scene.

and her parents will arrive soon.
they all knew that.

arms, those arms, wrapped about
porridge and kippers which sent
the scent wheeling past her nostrils.
she sighed the goodness of England
and smiled with the frozen air.
parents, chattels, will come about now --
'gulls, bring Oma* in your beak.'
but the bird shrieked to ignore.
and the train slid through.

these hundreds of children
swaddled in worsted
bore wide black eyes
which saw heaven as a
single marshmallow.
her parents were shortly to come.
they all knew that.

steadily, stealthily, time fell, never to recover itself,
leaves rose up juicing their greens
because trees stand up to war.

her mother/father photograph
her violin
her new leather shoes
breathing beneath a pillow
were used to placate other
weeping girls
while she wept on.

her parents should be coming
but something had re-routed them
onto a different set of tracks.

now, many years on
and I move around the very
same trees.
I carry inside a seed
which has grown as a seed should
when I yield it up
and give it the chance of life
I shall wonder
whereabouts my Oma lies.

in its eyes
in its fears
in its past.

* Oma - grandmother

Charlotte Peploe was born in 1961 and trained in Textile Design. She has worked as a waitress, secretary, fashion writer and administrator for the Jewish Institute. She is now a teacher, a Vietnamese Worker and a mother.

SAEED AHMED

My Journey to England

When I was thirteen years old I lived in Somalia in a town called Buro. In my family I had my mum, my dad and my brothers and sister. We were a happy family and Buro was a nice little town. People in the town were working and they were happy.

Suddenly, everything changed. We had a war in Somalia. People were fighting and killing each other. Many people were leaving the country because they were not safe in Somalia. Many people from my town, too, were going; some were killed and some lost their house and family.

One day, my dad came home looking very sad. Mum said, 'you don't look very happy. What's the matter?' My father replied, 'we have to leave this house because it is not safe here.' My mother started crying, 'how can we leave this house? We built it and our children were born here.' My father said, 'we have to go to another country to save the children.' My mother agreed, and started packing all our clothes and some food in bags.

It was a sunny and hot day. We left our home at ten o'clock in the morning. We were all crying. We took a last look at our house and started our journey. I saw that many other families were also leaving. We caught a bus from Buro to Ethiopia.

It was a long, hard journey which lasted about seven hours. We were all tired and hungry. My father took us to a hotel. People who wanted to go to Europe or England came to stay in this hotel. It was a nice hotel, warm and comfortable. We stayed there for a week to sort out our passports and visas and plane tickets.

We were all sad because we were thinking about the house and our friends. I had some nice friends in my school. We used to play football together. I don't know what has happened to them, but I still think of them.

Finally, my father sorted everything out and we were ready to come to England. First we caught a plane to Sudan. We had to wait for one hour there. After that we got on a big plane for England. I was very excited because this was my first time on a plane. I was scared but after half an hour a lady gave us some food and drink and that made me feel better. We ate our food but I did not eat much because it was different from the food we were used to. After half an hour I fell asleep.

I woke up at Heathrow Airport. I heard the pilot saying, 'this is Heathrow in London'. We came to the waiting area. They asked us for our passports. We handed them over and they looked at them. Then we sat in the waiting room and I saw an Ethiopian woman who had lost her passport and was crying. After half an hour they let us go. We caught a bus to Sheffield.

When we came to Sheffield we stayed in a hotel. It was a nice hotel and it was warm. We stayed there for a week and then they gave us a house. I went to a school called Earl Marshall in Sheffield. There, I learned English. A year later, I moved to Bristol but my family stayed there. I moved with my brother, who goes to the University of the West of England.

Now I live in Bristol and go to St George Community School. I would like to go back to Somalia as soon as possible when I finish at school, I hope. The war in Somalia has stopped, now everything is normal. I would love to see my house again. It might have been destroyed, but I hope it is alright.

The Long Journey of Belonging

From Berlin to Bristol in three generations

I was born in Cambridge in 1942. We moved to Aldermaston when I was eight, near the new Atomic Weapons Research Establishment, and then to Reading when I was twelve. My father died very suddenly when I was 14, and both my brother (three years younger than me) and I went to boarding school as a result of this. When I left school, I had a 'year out' and then went to university.

It felt a fairly ordinary British upbringing, except for the awareness that my family was a bit different -- my parents were Jewish refugees from Nazi Germany, having escaped to England in 1937.

This 'differentness' exhibited itself in several ways. My parents had foreign accents and mispronounced a few words from time to time. Occasional visitors with much thicker accents came and talked German with them, and we were very bored as we did not understand. We realised they often talked about mysterious things in the past -- but not for long. My parents mostly refused to speak German at home, and we were brought up speaking only English. German was only used to hide things from us children, so we knew when there were secrets to find out.

In many ways my parents were less staid than many English people of the time -- for instance, my mother would always swim with us rather than just watch, and she wore trousers when few women did. This admirable quality had its 'downside', though. When she complained in a very loud voice about poor service in shops and department stores, my brother and I would hide in embarrassment at the next counter and pretend we were with someone else.

My schoolfriends found our family's food somewhat unusual, but after eyeing it apprehensively, found it really tasty. My mother adapted recipes from Germany, England and elsewhere, whatever was cheap yet nourishing, as we were pretty poor for most of the time. (This was partly because my parents had to support my grandparents as well as our family, and partly because my father's work as a research physicist was not very well paid.) Food was always adequate, but even now I feel compelled to eat up what is on my plate. Clothes were in short supply and my school uniform coat was my only coat -- but I only minded when I had to wear home-made skirts from furnishing material and other children laughed at me for wearing 'old sacks'.

I always thought of our family as very small (my parents, my brother and one set of grandparents). Only later did I realise that, but for the Holocaust, I would have been part of a large extended Jewish family. I might well not have liked them all, but that is another matter! I was fascinated with other children's talk of cousins, aunts and uncles, as we had none -- until my cousin turned up when he was 29 and I was 19. My parents had missed him when he arrived on the kindertransport in 1939, and he had been brought up by foster parents in Wales.

At least there were my grandparents on my father's side. My grandfather only ever communicated with us by waving his stick and shouting at us in German, which we didn't understand. But my grandmother sang us 'The Last Rose of Summer' in a cracked voice and made wonderful apfeltorte. In Cambridge they lived in a damp little house with an earthenware sink and an outside toilet. After my grandfather's death, my grandmother was rehoused in a 'prefab' on the outskirts of Cambridge, and much later in

a Jewish elderly persons' home in London. We visited her there and became aware, for the first time, of the Jewish food laws -- eating strange meals of spinach-and-egg, or schnitzel with lemon tea to avoid milk and meat mixing at the same meal. All the residents were refugees from central Europe, and spoke a mixture of German and heavily accented English which my mother nicknamed 'immigranto'.

We also saw for the first time some of the trappings of Jewish religious life, such as 'mezzuzahs' (little doorpost containers of verses from the first five books of the Bible) and 'menorahs' (seven-branched candle-sticks). Jewish religion was even further from our family's experience than the Church of England -- in fact, my mother had had us christened in the latter, to be truly British and help our assimilation! I went to a church secondary school as the most academically suitable, and was puzzled by the pictures we had to copy of Jews with long flowing head-dresses. These Jews didn't seem to be the same at all as my relatives.

My parents tried as hard as they could to assimilate into their new haven and country of asylum. As parents are so often judged by their children's behaviour, we always had to be on our best behaviour outside the home -- with the consequence that we were often pretty awful at home. It was hard to feel that we really belonged when we had to try so hard and behave so well to be acceptable.

I was at university when Enoch Powell made his pronouncements about sending immigrants, including second generation immigrants, 'back home'. As a fervent anti-racist, I realised this was terrible news for black people born in Britain. However, it was only when a good friend of mine, with an Indian father and a Danish mother, said to me, 'where is Enoch Powell going to send me -- to India or Denmark?' that I realised this would apply to me, too. I could be sent 'back' to Germany, a country I hardly thought of as mine after what had happened. Until then, I

had seen myself as 'ordinary British', not as a 'second generation immigrant', an experience parallel to that of many black people.

I had actually been to Germany, during my 'gap year' before university. My parents never went back and also took pains to avoid Germany whenever they travelled to Europe, even if it meant taking a longer route. They had British passports and, if asked about their origins or their good German, would say they had studied in Berlin.

I wanted to see this terrible country with my own eyes, and ask many questions. I also felt that I had a choice -- to continue to shun all Germans, reasonable enough in the circumstances -- or to try to start afresh with my own generation, to prevent anything similar ever happening again. I wanted to do the latter. I was fortunate to be able to stay for two months with a fine elderly couple who had suffered greatly during the Nazi times for their stand, without even being Jewish. However, it never entered my head to think of Germany as 'my' country. It certainly was not.

As a child, I had heard some of the most exciting stories from my mother -- how they had stuffed anti-Nazi leaflets down the toilet as the Gestapo knocked loudly at the door; how they worked on dangerous missions in the Underground Movement; how they corresponded in code to negotiate a job in England; how my father's passport was confiscated as he prepared to leave; how he got it back and jumped on the next train out of Berlin for Paris; how my mother wrapped up their life and followed 36 hours later, and finally how they found their feet in England.

As an adult, I wanted my mother to write her memoirs so that I had a fuller picture of the context of the Holocaust and what happened to my family in it. However, life was busy after my father died, especially as my mother suddenly had to work full-time as a college lecturer (as an immigrant she had not been allowed to work, despite her professional qualifications, and later she had stayed at home with us children, as was conventional then). In any case, she could not face talking about it in full.

It was only when she retired and suffered a massive heart attack, that the memoirs became an urgent task. After a couple of false starts (she did not enjoy writing and also found it distressing), I took a week's holiday and we sat with a tape recorder while I plied her with questions. It took over a year to edit the conversations into a book for her 70th birthday.

Here are some excerpts from her memoirs, entitled *We Kept Our Heads -- Personal memories of being Jewish in Nazi Germany and making a new home in England*, by Dodo Liebmann:

ABOUT BEING JEWISH

My family was a typical Jewish German middle-class family, and the society I grew up in was almost exclusively Jewish. Though ghettos had been abolished long ago, and in Berlin Jews did not actually live very close together, they preferred certain parts of the city. In spite of not living very near other Jews, my family mixed socially almost exclusively with Jews. Anti-Semitism was widespread, and I was brought up in the belief that only among Jews could we consider ourselves safe.

We considered ourselves firstly German and only secondly Jewish; we were very patriotic. After all, Jews had lived in Germany for many generations. So the Nazis' persecution of the Jews came as a big shock to most Jews.

Like many Jewish homes in Germany, our home was not orthodox. We kept the high festivals, the Day of Atonement and New Year's Day, and that was more or less all. Of course, we had Jewish religious instruction at school, while the others had Christian religious instruction. In my school, almost half the girls were Jewish, so we parted into two roughly equal groups.

NAZI TIMES

Hitler became Chancellor on January 31st, 1933, and soon afterwards all other political parties were made illegal. There were all sorts of other restrictions and laws that crept in, as the Nazis gained more power.

I had always had endless discussions about social problems with my friends at school. Later, at university, I drifted into a very left-wing circle of friends. The fact that it did not matter whether we were Jews or Gentiles made it a great attraction. I became a member of the Communist Party only in 1933, when Hitler took over.

Sometimes I had to collect or deliver clandestine news sheets. One day I had to take some material to work with me for delivery. Someone told me, just as a piece of gossip, that the police were searching the factory for underground literature. I went straight to the toilet, stuffed everything down there, and flushed. Nothing much happened, and I had to wait in agony for the cistern to fill up, to flush again; now it went down without leaving a trace. By this time, the Nazi girls who always helped on these occasions, had arrived in full force inside the toilet, hammering at the door of my cubicle. When I eventually opened the door, I was accused of having disposed of something and of having flushed twice. I agreed I had flushed twice, as I liked to leave the toilet clean for the next person to use. I must have escaped being caught by less than a minute. When I came out, I was searched thoroughly, but of course I was now quite clean. The matter was reported, and the officer in charge of the action came and questioned me closely, but I gave the same answer. They searched everwhere, but found nothing.

I was unemployed at the end of 1934. Jobs were really difficult to get in the 1930s, and if you were Jewish as well, it was almost hopeless. Gert and I were intending to get married sometime, and he had the brilliant idea that I should edit a monthly journal of abstracts for the radio industry. I started the journal in January 1935 and ran it for 18 months. I couldn't advertise or publicise the journal, as this would have got the 'Schriftumkammer' and other Nazi organisations on my trail. The 'Schriftumkammer' was an official body which looked after everything that was published in Germany under the Nazis. If you were not of pure German descent, you were not allowed to publish anything -- certainly not if you were Jewish. In spite of this, I had quite a good response, and most of the university libraries in the whole of Europe, including the British Museum, had copies. I don't know how everyone got to hear of it.

About half way through this period, I had an offer from the Technical University in Berlin. They said, 'look, we have started something very similar to yours, and we're already six months behind. Would you mind coming here and doing it for us, and we'll pay you.' It seemed that anything could be arranged, they were so keen to get me; in the end I could think of no more reasons for saying no. And then the inevitable question came. 'Sind Sie eine Volksgenossin?' -- a peculiar phrase meaning, 'are you Aryan?' I said no, and the man went beetroot-red and said, 'there is nothing more to be said about it.'

I can still remember walking along the Charlottenburger Chaussee outside the Technical University and literally having a bitter taste in my mouth. It was so appalling that just because we were of the wrong colour, creed or birth, we couldn't do what we were really perfectly fitted to do.

I continued the journal on my own. Just after a year, the Schriftumkammer started to write to me, but I never answered them. When the letters became more frequent, and demanded an answer, I just stopped publication, because I didn't want to go to prison or concentration camp.

After 1933, many friends and relatives were beginning to leave Germany. Quite a number of people just disappeared; they usually didn't even say goodbye, but very often they visited you, brought you a present of chocolates, or something a little unusual, and then you knew, 'ah, another one going.'

We were in a very wide circle of friends, but the only ones I kept up with were the Jews who went out of Germany.

The others wouldn't write to you after the Nazis came into power because they were afraid of endangering their lives.

EMIGRATION

Gert and I had been thinking of emigrating for about two years before we actually left. In 1936 there was an advertisement in an English periodical; it seemed to be the job for Gert. He wrote to our friends in London, who submitted his application and all his papers (left there from a previous visit) to the firm, who then asked him to come over for interview. He arranged that the answer be sent, not to us, but to our London friends, because we were frightened that if it came to Germany, the letter might be opened. We had arranged a code, so when we got a letter from our friends saying 'the ammeter is working satisfactorily, with one second swinging time and 500 milliamps current consumption', we knew it meant that the job was OK, with a contract for one year, and £500 a year salary.

My family said goodbye to me. Why my sister and brother-in-law never tried to get out, I don't know; my sister died only the year after I left. They just said goodbye, and hoped everything would be alright; I expect my mother hoped I would be able to fetch her afterwards, which then wasn't possible.

FIRST IMPRESSIONS OF ENGLAND

When we arrived in England at the beginning of 1937, everyone marvelled at the way we were completely normal -- and had not been influenced by the Nazi ideology. Most of the other refugees had persecution mania -- they didn't dare to say a loud word even when they had got safely to England. I think it was our political work that had kept us sane.

We had cakes and butter and real cocoa! The stuff we had bought as cocoa in Germany certainly wasn't cocoa. And the soap flakes here foamed and foamed -- I realised that the soap in Germany had also been adulterated. Our time in Cambridge was very nice; we tried to learn a bit of gardening, because both of us were town people, and hadn't a clue which plants were weeds and which were flowers. I learned to make jam, because we had so much fruit in the garden, and also did some bottling. I did all sorts of things, because I had nothing else to do, as the wife of the one who had the labour permit. I applied to work on my own account but the Home Office declined permission.

I found I fitted in very much better in England than in Germany, because people let me be. Although there were a lot of unwritten laws in England, too, you were allowed to deviate from the norm, as long as you didn't tread on your neighbours' toes. In Germany you had to do things a certain way, and that was that -- and I never felt really at home there.

My mother retired from Reading to London to be nearer old friends, and also to see more of me and my brother as we passed through London from time to time. When I moved to Bristol in 1968 with my job, she came to visit regularly. As she became more frail, she came less often but for longer periods. She got to know many of my friends and felt quite at home in Bristol -- she even considered moving here but thought she would find the hills difficult and that she would miss her friends. After a series of operations in 1989, she came to recuperate here but then relapsed and died in hospital in Bristol. Her funeral was held at Canford Lane, with my friends in attendance -- we later held a memorial meeting in London for her friends. She was 83.

I've lived in Bristol for nearly 30 years now, and it's my home. I married here -- to an unconventional but truly English man whose family found me quite 'unusual' for quite some time. Our daughter Anna was born in Bristol in 1979.

My working life has been varied, but with a thread running through it -- I have worked in a school, a day centre, victim support, probation, art therapy, mediation and conflict resolution, trying to increase my own and others' understanding of how any situation like the Holocaust can be prevented in the future. As part of this search, I became a Quaker twenty years ago.

I currently work part-time for Mediation UK, the national charity for mediation in the community, and part-time as art therapist for the Inner City Mental Health Team -- where most staff and many clients have similar stories to mine. They or their parents have come here from all parts of the world, either from necessity of circumstances or to seek a better life.

Anna, now just 18, has her own perspective: Like my mother, I try to start afresh with as little prejudice as possible. I think this is to do with my being a Quaker, but it has helped a lot in coming to terms with the Holocaust. I too have always had a small family -- Dodo being my only grandparent and dying when I was not quite ten -- and thinking that I may have had, or have, an extended Jewish family in Europe, but that I'll never really know, does kind of turn my stomach. With the number of Jewish emigrants, too, I could have relatives in America or somewhere ...

However, it's important to me to wipe the slate clean, and 'look for that of God in everyone' (Quaker saying), so much so that I am a lot less anti-German than many of my contemporaries (who perhaps don't have a personal link, so haven't thought so carefully).

I am sometimes in a quandary over whether I am half-Jewish or half-German, or neither. Dodo always said, 'I am not German, I am Jewish', and even forbade my mother buying a Volkswagen car! My mother is semi-Jewish and not really German at all. Traditionally, I am Jewish, this being hereditary through mothers only, but ironically I am often taken for being German because of my typical blonde hair and blue eyes. I am British, but not really proud to be, and seeing as I have so many labels to choose from and am a bad decision-maker, I just stay as 'Anna'.

Marian Liebmann has lived in Bristol for nearly 30 years, and regards it as her home. She is married with one daughter. She is of Jewish background, and became a Quaker 25 years ago. She currently works part-time for Mediation UK in mediation and conflict resolution, and also as art therapist for the Inner City Mental Health Team. She has written and edited several books on art therapy, mediation and conflict resolution, including Arts Approaches to Conflict, which brings these together. When not working, she enjoys swimming, walking, travel and being with friends.

Anna Coldham is an 18-year old techno cycle fascist, trying to hold down physics and photography A Levels. She participates in and helps to organise local and national Young Quaker events, has played in county orchestras and peace camped, and is currently trying to save the world.

In Principio

In principio
We, I, you, left
We arrived
In between
Worried about losing our identities
we kept our passports
... to confirm our worries

ELAINE KING

I've Always Felt Like a Parcel

I've always felt like a parcel. I can hear you asking why? Well, you see when I was nine, my mother sent for me. I came in the June and I was ten the following February. I remember I wore a blue suit which was two sizes too big for me.

It was a skirt and jacket, and I wore a hat, or did I have two large plaits with blue ribbons in my hair? I wore short white socks and new black shiny shoes. I remember walking across the tarmac when I left Jamaica. I never looked back. I was so thin, I felt so lonely, I was leaving all I ever knew. I sat next to a white boy who was going to school, he tried to make me eat, but I couldn't eat a single thing.

I was leaving Mum, Auntie Nita, Sister Virgie, Mamie, Mackie, Paulette and Marie, Baby G, my brother Frank, Laurent and Black Boy, Uncle Herman, Uncle Hosea, Miss Florence, Bev and Jimmy.

I arrived in England. Funny, I knew my mother straight away, only from her photograph. I couldn't call her Mum, I called her Aunt Birdie. Why? Because the only mother I ever knew was left behind in J.A. It was a long drive to Bristol. When I reached Grosvenor Road I thought the houses were factories. I couldn't understand why people lived in factories.

It was twenty-five years later that I fully realised why I could never remember my mother's smile, no mother's kiss, no mother's hug. Twenty-five years to realise that I'd lost so much. I was lost in primary school. I knew more than they did, it seems I was ahead, about a year later they caught up or was it I slowed down, I never really knew.

In secondary school during domestic science, the teacher said bring mince meat for the next lesson. It was close to Christmas time. I went to the butcher and got my mince meat. No one told me there was sweet mince meat and savoury mince meat. I was totally mortified.

I was head girl in my last year at school, only the second black girl to be so. I was brilliant at commerce. My teacher told me to get a job in banking or insurance. Alas, I couldn't get in. Only NatWest offered me a chance, but only if I was willing to move to London. I was 16 and very insecure, so since then I've been in Bristol.

I've always felt like a parcel and now I want to be posted back home.

Elaine King is 42, is qualified in social work but works in the voluntary sector and is very committed to the value people get from volunteering. She herself does a lot of voluntary work in her community. She loves dancing to Revival music, reading black authors and others and hopes to travel and/or settle in Africa or Jamaica. She has one son and grandson and her mother went back to live in Jamaica three years ago and is happily settled there.

Dearest Gogo

May I call you Gogo, the Kalenjin word for grandmother? Do let me know which you prefer.

I am writing to you to try to put into words my feelings about meeting you for the first time. I can hardly believe that I am your oldest grandchild. Nothing could have prepared me for what I experienced last summer. For thirty-four years I have been the only African child adopted into an English Quaker family. I have had very little knowledge about my past.

Although I knew my mother had died soon after my birth, I discovered only last year that my father Matayo was alive and living in a remote village in western Kenya. Imagine my surprise to learn not only that he had remarried, but that I have seven half-sisters and four half-brothers!

On the day of our meeting I was so nervous. I did not know what to expect. Previously relatives and friends in England had warned me about the dangers of visiting an isolated area. 'Beware of the tribal elders ... Be warned -- they will demand a high bride price ... Didn't you know that a black American woman tried to do the same thing two years ago? She was seized and circumcised against her will ... The area you want to visit could be too risky.'

I was prepared to encounter suspicion, coolness, even hostility. I was petrified. But something inside me pressed me on.

A missionary friend who had known me as an infant kindly offered to take me, my husband and two children back to the village I originated from. We got lost several times as there was no road. We passed in the shadows of the towering Nandi Rock, which tribes used for human sacrifices over thirty years ago. Our journey was temporarily interrupted when crowds of women and children streamed on to our path, carrying food and clothing to the young men in the forest. Unbeknown to us this was the year of the male circumcision which took place every five years.

After two hours I was glad to get out of our vehicle and walk the final part of the journey. It had been a long, hot and dusty drive. We walked down into the valley and up the other side. The hillside was covered in maize swaying in the heat. When I looked up into the sunlight, I saw two women running towards me, arms outstretched. I know now that they were Damaizy, my father's second wife and her first-born child, Wangeri. Their faces were lit by the sunshine and their smiles and hugs made me feel instantly welcome. We walked back in the home compound, a clearing with two separate mud-walled houses, and although my father was not at home at that time, I met you.

Grandmother, your blindness means your family were your eyes. We could not speak the same language but your tears as you kissed my fingers humbled me. You held me. I heard you sing. I heard you laugh. We all danced. You fed us. My children, your great-grandchildren played with their Kalenjin cousins among the lush green vegetation.

For a time I imagined I was a young Kalenjin girl helping to take care of the cattle with the older children. We roamed the Nandi Hills looking for new pastures. We guarded that which would be our children's with the passing years - cattle, land, family.

Suddenly I feel proud of who I am and where I come from. I feel privileged to be the centre of such celebration. I hope we will meet again. We can walk together in the Nandi Hills and you will whisper, 'Let

the vision of Kenya grow within you.'

Thank you for accepting me into your life. Your oldest Kalenjin grand-daughter has at last returned.

Kageha Jeruto Marshall is originally from Kenya. She came to live in England in 1972 at the age of eleven. She spent six years in Kenya and five years in Uganda. Kageha was trans-racially adopted by a Quaker family as a baby, and she retraced her steps to her roots in western Kenya in 1995. Kageha was able to meet her natural father and his family for the first time in over 30 years.

Kageha now lives in Bristol with her husband and two daughters. In 1996 she took part in a film project with HTV as part of a series about Bristol families.

This account of her personal journey is in letter form, written to her natural grandmother whom she met for the first time. Although her grandmother was blind and there was a language barrier, she was able to welcome Kageha and her family into the family home.

Kageha's father and second wife

"Most of my mother's family were killed in the Holocaust, but my Russian grandmother arrived on a train with one jewel pinned to her hat. She bought a house in England with that jewel ..."

Bristol Jewish lady

Mrs Sheik: I first came to London from Karachi. I had a really good time, I've had no problems in England and have been here 22 years. I had a friend who helped me out a lot, we went shopping together so I had no real problems. I did work for a short time in Bristol, at Grantham sewing uniforms. The language wasn't too much of a problem, my daughter worked with me and she helped me out. Then my health deteriorated and I gave up.

We do go back to visit Pakistan, and I would like to live there, but what kind of life would it be for me on my own? My husband is dead and my children are here, but if even one of them wanted to go back with me to live, I would consider it. We have a house in Pakistan and usually go for two or three months at a time. Karachi is a big town, it has a lot of facilities, good houses. I would like to go back because half the family are out there.

Anon: Southmead used to be the one hospital for births before St Michael's maternity hospital was built 21 years ago. My daughter was born there on the same day the hospital was opened, and she was on television, both BBC and HTV. She was one of the first babies born when the hospital was finished. Then on the 21st anniversary my grand-daughter was born at St Michael's. It was good. Everyone came, what's his name the Lord Mayor was there, it was a good party. I've now been in England nearly forty years. We first went to Oxford, my husband was doing English there. After that we came to Bristol and it's now been 35 years. In Oxford, there were no Asian families. We moved to Totterdown where there were three other families. It was good to have other Asians around.

Anon: My uncle was here and his wife and also my husband lived in the house. The children wouldn't go out because everywhere there were white people and we couldn't see anyone of our own colour. During the day, when my husband was around, the time passed happily but then he would go to work and I would be alone in the house. I couldn't speak any English, but now I can go out and get by with my English. My husband used to go shopping with me. There was a shop in City Road we would go to; we would also go to the city farm, because we needed to get halal meat and we would get the chicken ourselves and slaughter them in the house. We found the place by chance. I used to enjoy just walking around and looking. It was one of these occasions: we heard chickens, we asked the lady if she would sell them to us, and so every two or three weeks we went to the farm to buy one.

The first mosque was in Totterdown and at that time there were more Asians living in Totterdown. In those days, it didn't really matter what kind of Muslim you were; all the Muslims helped each other out, and because there was only one mosque all the Muslims would get together to pray on Fridays. No problem at the beginning, although now there are many mosques all over. In the old days, you were happy to meet another Muslim and it didn't matter which denomination you were from.

I have four children. My first experience of an English hospital was when my daughter was about to be born. It was my first child and I was very young. I didn't know how you have a baby. No one told me, because we were alone; at about four months into the pregnancy I started feeling sick, got a fever, I couldn't cook, I was in a bad way. I didn't have a clue what had happened or what the reason was and

SABERA BHAM

for many days I craved apples, unripe apples from a tree.

My husband couldn't understand why I was this way. He took me to the doctor and said I had been sick for many days, and had been getting upset. 'What's wrong with her?' The doctor gave me a check up and said I was four months pregnant. My husband was very happy. I started crying lots and lots and asked, 'how am I having a child?' He kept saying don't fear, and went to get me some unripe apples. They tasted really good, it reminded me of back home. I went into hospital two weeks before the baby was due. I cried a lot. It was hard to know what was going on, as I couldn't speak English. The nurses would ask if I was in pain and I would say no. One nurse had told me that as soon as I get pains I should tell them. The nurses kept asking what was wrong, why are you crying, and I would say I was thinking of my mother and missing her.

My mother would usually have her children during the night when all of us were asleep. In the morning we would see a baby lying next to her and ask where it had come from, and she would say, 'I got him from the clinic'. Even young children these days realise they don't come from the clinic. My grandson is 2$^{1}/_{2}$ and I said to him, 'your mummy has gone to get the baby from the hospital. He said, 'no, she has got it in the stomach.' The children know these things now.

It was hard not knowing the language. I started buying a few things and I got to know the shops and know that this road went here and that road went there, and I won't get lost. I used to carry my address with me so that if I did get lost I could show it to someone.

At first, English people would stare at Asian people, looking at the way we spoke and the way we walked and what we wore. When we would go out, they would look at our clothes and the colours and say they were nice. That's all changed now. In those days you put something down and the next day it would still be there, but these days they steal it from your hands. The English used to be good people with love and they would look out for one another. Now they go 'look Paki'. Many people are bad and many are good, but today's generation is not good.

[Contributed by members of the **Barton Hill Asian Women's Group** talking to **Jamila Yousaf**]

"We women meet up regularly and talk about how we got here,
about our past life ... one young woman told us
that she was running from the fighting with a sack of rice on her back.
All she knew was that she had to get to the port to flee.
When she got to the port, her sack of rice
had been emptied by bullet holes —
she had no food,
but the sack of rice had saved her life."

Bristol Somali lady

"I came to Bristol as a small boy ...
I used to wander around completely disoriented,
never knowing where I was or what time of day it was ...
you see, I couldn't see the stars every night or the sun every day —
there was always a thick low layer of grey cloud ...
on a tropical island away from the city
you always looked to the sky to tell the time."

St Paul's resident, originally from Jamaica

Cry for the Nation

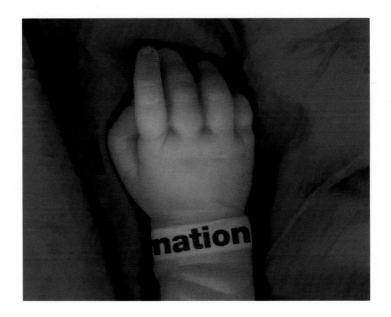

I search the faces
The faces of the people
They who are afraid of the past
The present and the future
I watch the ones who cannot sing
They who have forgotten
How to express the inner workings of the heart
I witness the self-destruction
The mis-use and abuse of power
I see the self-loathing

The anger and the pain
The sorrow and the hurt --
I sigh as they all go by
These unloved, lost and lonely children
They are jewels who have lost their sparkle
And no matter how hard I try to help
I cannot move --
Overcome by my own emotions
I flow with tears
As I cry for the Nation.

51

Learning the 'English Way'

It started in Kingston, Jamaica. I was staying with a cousin of mine, and that is where my future was being planned. It had been settled for me to attend a school of hairdressing. Then, out of the blue, there was a letter from my mother telling me that her brother, my uncle, was in England and had been there a few years. He said in the letter 'why don't you send Joyce over to England for a few years?' as they would be returning in two or three years' time and I could return with them. My mother said yes. In Jamaica, and maybe here as well sometimes, they don't really ask the children -- the children go along with the decisions.

So my mother phoned my brother and told him to get everyone to help me get ready for England. And that was that. What did I think about this? Nothing! When I look back on it now, I think to myself -- why didn't I just say 'no'? Look how far England is from Jamaica -- and I knew nothing about England except what was taught in schools. I was never told how cold it was! Or about snow!

I went over to my brother's house and everything had been set up for me to go. I didn't even see the money that had been paid. None of this was because I was a bad girl -- I was the only sister, the only daughter. They were trying to do something for me, but without asking me! I will never forget the party my family and friends had for me before I was to travel. So many prayers were said for me. I was so foolish, when I look back, but you didn't rebel, you didn't say 'I don't want to go ...'

I travelled to England by boat. It was horrible. When I look back and watch all these things on television about black people travelling from one country to another -- it was the same for me, I didn't know a soul. The journey took 16 days and I was sick all the way. I could only drink black coffee. We got to England and I spent two days sleeping on a train. I had no idea where I was going, except to stay with my uncle, his wife and my cousin.

I was shocked by England. All the houses looked like great big ships. I had never seen houses like that before, only bungalows and huts. I went to live in London at first. I was cold and homesick. I wrote to my mother to say I wanted to go home. I didn't have any warm clothes, so my cousin, who was a tailor, made me a fleecy coat. But I was lucky, some people didn't have anything. You could see people coming off the boat in their shirt sleeves. Yes, it was summer, but it was cold for us. I just couldn't get warm, I used to leave my pyjama top on underneath my clothes. I never got warm, it was in my bones.

In London a job was there waiting for me, because of my uncle. But the distressing part of it was that I had never worked before. I was taking a role of a child, I did what I was told! When I watch my children now and the things they do ... So, I started work at St Pancras Hospital -- they were desperate to fill the jobs. I thought I could earn some money quickly and then return. If you talk to other people from the West Indies, that's what they will say. 'We're just here to work for two years, and then go back,' but it didn't work like that at all.

I missed Jamaica. I missed seeing the stars. In Jamaica you could look up at night and there would be the stars and a dark blue sky. You could see the stars run across the sky. I used to look for them as a child: a star would run with a tail. When we first came here there was a joke among the English children -- they would ask you the time because they thought you could read it from the sky. But I didn't realise that because where I'm from we all had watches! I

never knew what was going on until another black lady said they were making fun of me!

I missed my home food. It's different now, but then there was only potatoes -- I don't remember eating rice then at all. I missed picking fruit from the trees. You could go into the back garden and get fruit. Here you had to buy everything and always go to the shops, which was a problem because they didn't want to serve you. They would put the money on the counter because they didn't want to put it in your hand. They weren't all like that, just a couple of shops. Because, you see, being black, that was a problem. And you went on the bus, and nobody would sit down by you. Not ever. We weren't warned of this, nobody told us. Being Jamaican, we were brought up to do everything 'like the English', my gosh, you could never find a child in Jamaica, unless desperately poor, not eating correctly with a knife and fork. You were brought up in the 'English way'. We didn't know anything else. Now today, I think before I die I want to go to Africa to see their tradition. In Jamaica we knew nothing about our roots. Nothing at all.

My future husband came to Bristol as all his relatives were here. I had met him on the boat coming over. Eventually I invited him to meet my uncle -- and that was that. My uncle said I must leave my job in London and go and live in Bristol as the man is the breadwinner. In the beginning, life was rough in Bristol. We moved five times before we were able to buy a house. Not everyone who came from the West Indies was poor. I wasn't. Dad was well off, he was well-travelled and had lots of business. In coming to England I was pushed into that kind of life where you share a stove with three other people -- this little ring for you, that little ring for you. Dreadful, dreadful, dreadful. My husband's cousin showed me the places to go and ask about jobs. Great big Southmead Hospital -- I walked straight in there and asked for a job. And because I was young, clean and looked them straight in the eyes, they asked me in and they asked me to apply properly and to sign my name. One of the sisters said 'Oh you write very nicely!' -- she was very surprised. I waited and waited to hear from them, and got a job three months later. I was 20 years in that job.

Now I feel more relaxed here. You build your life on what you have, and I'm not going to let anybody else or colour stop me from getting what I want. I am so strong that going into groups of people where I am the only black person doesn't bother me. I walk into 'nice' places, expensive restaurants, I know what to do -- to eat like anybody else, but I never look at anyone. If I look at anyone, it's as if I'm scared, so I walk in as if I belong to this place as well. I'm very, very strong, and glad that I have overcome this -- I have lots of friends that are English, white and different nationalities.

But I never settled. I talk about nothing else but that I am going home. Am I really going home? It's so difficult. I wish I had gone when my children were very small. But it didn't work out like that -- they were born here, but I pine to go home. I retired last year, and went home to make up my mind. I have a house in Jamaica that belonged to my parents. I am divorced, and so I have worked to bring up my children properly and then to return. I have always gone shopping -- and if I buy a blouse I will buy something else to put in the trunk -- to go back. I'm always putting back things. Just the other day I said to myself -- some of those things you have in boxes you should take out and leave. You are now over 60! All these years I'll have one tablecloth out for the table and four upstairs in the trunk. It's madness!

That's how my life has been -- split. All the time looking in shops and thinking of things to put back. Because when you go home, you won't have that money. I think every West Indian or foreigner, especially black people, will have something put aside, that says 'I will return'. You see, we weren't welcome. You always feel you must do it right. You must dress properly to tell them you are clean and have nice clothes, always. You are never free from that. The children had to be turned out properly. Everyone does this, but it was a burden for us, because the white people were always ready to say 'look at them, dirty, filthy.' I have heard it. But if you're too nicely dressed it's a problem again -- 'they come here and get all the jobs.' We are never right. Some were jealous if your children were too well dressed. We were always busy, trying to please the world. David, my second son, once was coming home with his white friend, and I could hear him say to the little boy, 'oh, come in, my house doesn't smell.' And that little boy's house did smell. So that was it -- because you were black, the children thought you were dirty. I just laugh about it now.

But life was hard for us when we came. Nobody would speak to you. But I don't blame them! In England it was white people all around. And out of the blue, an influx of black people! What hurt me was the government inviting us over to work, and I just wonder if they told people in the papers or on tv that this was going to happen, and why we were coming? Why did people keep saying we shouldn't have come except for the jobs! But they, the English, didn't like seeing you around at all. I used to go to the doctors or go on the bus and children and even babies would stretch out their hands to play with my little one, and the mothers would snatch their little baby hands away.

Joyce Anderson, born in 1931, worked as a health care assistant. She has four grandchildren and loves the cinema, music, travelling, reading and entertaining.

Life After Vietnam

Everyone has a different story, Thong. When did you come to England? How did you get here?

I arrived in England in May, 1979. I was rescued with my family by a British ship and they took us to Hong Kong and after three weeks we were flown here and lived in a reception centre near Christchurch. We lived there for about 4½ months, we were then offered a house in Bath and have been living there ever since.

And how long was your journey on the boat? Were you frightened?

My family and I were on a boat for a few days. I wasn't frightened because I was below deck and didn't really see anything, but there were many hundreds of people on the boat, about 25 metres long and five metres wide. Very tiny. I came with my wife and two children.

You ended up in Britain because you were rescued by a British ship -- but other member escaped and were picked up by French and American ships?

My six brothers and sister escaped in 1975 when there was an exodus of Vietnamese. They were accepted by the French and American governments, so now I have three brothers in France and three in America. But I have no regret at all, because I believe in fate. And life in England is slower than in the USA, it is difficult to become rich but at least you have time to relax, you don't have to run to keep up with the pace of life. People become very selfish and ruthless in the USA, running after money and becoming mean.

So, now you are in England. What was it like to come here?

My first impression of England was when I went to the Sopley Reception Centre. They took us by coach from Heathrow Airport. We stopped at some service station, and I looked around ... the weather was very cold, we didn't have the right clothes. When we had boarded the plane to come to England, we had nothing. Some people didn't even have shoes! On the boat you could hardly breathe, it was so stuffy and hot, people got rid of their clothes and when the ship rescued us, I looked around and all our clothing had disappeared. When I climbed up the rope ladder to the rescue ship I had just a T-shirt and shorts, everything else had gone. Everyone was in a similar situation. We all thought the big ship would provide things, but it was a British cargo ship transporting goods from India to England.

They didn't expect to be rescuing people from the sea! It was by chance and their humanitarianism. They didn't have food for us. We had what they had -- they didn't just rescue one boat, but two, so there were more than a thousand of us on board. We were lucky to have something to eat. We slept on the deck and were on the boat for about four days.

We came to Hong Kong and after a delay we were finally allowed to dock, we were taken to a prison. Other people were taken to a camp, but because we were rescued by a British ship we went to a prison building. We stayed there for three weeks, they didn't allow us to go out. They didn't take everyone at once out of the prison to fly to England. They took people step by step and we were nearly the last. We managed to stay together as a family. My children were six and nearly seven years old. They knew everything that was happening, and my

daughter wrote it all down few years later.

Have you been back to Vietnam?

I have been back twice. I went with my family, I have only in-laws living there now. I felt very emotional to see my country. I am very attached to it. I was in the army and I have given blood for my country. We lost the war and now we have to live in exile here. For people who were poor in Vietnam, life in England is paradise. For me, it's not the same, as I had an easy life in Vietnam. I was a pharmacist and lived quite comfortably -- here my standard of living has dropped quite a lot. But with poor people from Vietnam, their standard of living has improved a lot.

And what do you feel now, living in the West, about all the media reports here of the Vietnam War?

The media have been very unfair towards the South Vietnamese. They show on the television the cruelty of the South Vietnamese army and the cruelty of the Americans. They never show the cruelty of the communist troops -- it is unfair. I blame, frankly speaking, the whole anti-war campaign in England and America. I blame the media, John Lennon, Jane Fonda, Joan Baez ... they were stupid. John Lennon and Yoko Ono posed naked and slept on a bed to protest against the war in Vietnam. They didn't understand anything about it. They didn't know about all the suffering and re-education camps -- I was imprisoned for nearly three years.

You see, before the fall of South Vietnam, people around the world supported the communists but afterwards they saw people like me risk their lives to leave, so they then had some idea of what the communist government was like. I was a pharmacist and I was thrown into prison, and the most frightening thing was that they didn't sentence you. You were put in prison and never knew if you would come out. You had to wait to see if the government thought you were 'good enough' to be released -- otherwise, you stayed. Ex-prisoners were then useless. Nobody wanted you. Now the government has opened its eyes.

Many people in South Vietnam are very well educated. I remember talking to poor cyclo riders, bare-footed who were Maths and English teachers before being thrown into 're-education' camps ...

When I went back to Vietnam I travelled by cyclo [rickshaw] and talked to the riders. Most of them are not peasants. They are well educated, officers of the South Vietnamese army and interpreters. They are very proud. When I offered them money -- more than they charged -- they refused to take it. They knew it was tough to make money abroad, too, for me. Only uneducated people in Vietnam think life is easy abroad and that money grows on trees.

Some Vietnamese have gone back. Would that be difficult for you?

Could I go back? The Vietnamese government allow only people like myself to go back and live over the age of 60. But the people now in the Hong Kong camps are being forced to re-patriate, because they are not political refugees but economic ones. Therefore no one will accept them. They are now forced to go back. The Vietnamese government did not use intellectuals before -- they now know they need grey matter! It is the brain that controls the movement of the body, not the muscle ... if you only use stupid people to run the country, as the Vietnamese have being doing until a few years ago, the country will always be behind.

Now they know they have to use new technology and brainy people. They cannot use people who are just members of the party. The communist regime didn't want intelligent people, because intelligent people ask questions. But with people who are fanatics, they don't ask, they just follow. But now the Government has opened its eyes and is using people with brains. It's a bit late, but better late than never. Vietnam is about 30 years behind Thailand and Malaysia and about 50 years behind England! You can catch up -- Vietnamese are very hard-working and intelligent. We arrived here with nothing; now all my family work. My wife works for an electronics company and my son is a trainee doctor. Only six per cent of Vietnamese here are unemployed.

There are very few Vietnamese in Bristol. Do they feel isolated?

There are only 360 Vietnamese in the Bristol area. They are all working too hard to feel isolated, except, that is, for the elderly. I work from Monday to Friday and on Saturday I go shopping with my wife. I watch football. I have no time to be bored.

It's better to have a small community because in London, which has many Vietnamese, there is an unemployment rate of 60 per cent. Easy to understand! If you live in a small city and are unemployed your get bored; if you live in London surrounded by many unemployed like yourself -- it's fine, but you are a burden on the State! Every day you see others like yourself in the same situation. You are not isolated but every day you lose enthusiasm to look for work.

You are a Buddhist. Do you have a temple here?

I am a devout Buddhist but there is no temple in Bristol or in Bath, only in London. I have a magazine from the temple. I believe in Buddha, my son is a Buddhist, I'm not sure about my daughter. My wife has a shrine, but she is not that devout. My son went to a Buddhist temple in Thailand for ten days to live like a monk.

Does your son feel Vietnamese or British now? Because he came from Vietnam, but only as a child -- do you think he feels a conflict between the two?

My children are Vietnamese, but their thinking is 90 per cent British. There is a conflict between the two cultures but they know what is wrong and what is right. When my children visit Vietnam, they become truly Vietnamese, but then of course back in England they become British!

There is a very different way of thinking and a different philosophy between Vietnamese and British people -- between the East and the West -- the Vietnamese are very philosophical about life and accept Fate ...

My children think like British children, but they are Vietnamese too. I say to them that they must keep our culture because there are many good things in the Vietnamese culture. For example, they worship their parents and ancestors and look after each other. Parents in Vietnam are not friends, they are advisors, not like here. Children here think their parents are friends, yet they put their grandparents in nursing homes -- this would be a very cruel thing to do in Vietnam!

In Vietnam at six o'clock in the morning the streets and parks are full of old people walking, running, exercising -- doing martial arts. They are always out at night. Old people in England are invisible. It must be very difficult for older Vietnamese people here ...

Yes ... very, very hard -- they get bored to death. The weather, the language barrier ... so I used to organise parties and lunches for them.

And what about celebrating Tet [Vietnamese New Year]? Do you do that here? In Vietnam it's so lively with all the firecrackers going off like bombs!

We do celebrate it here -- and yet the Vietnamese government in the last few years has forbidden firecrackers!

Why have they been banned? Because they are dangerous?

No, because the Government says they are a waste of money!

People need to celebrate the New Year ...

Yes, the firecracker is lit to chase away the bad luck in

the next year and to welcome the good luck. The firecracker is vital for life! Tet is the same day as the Chinese New Year, and they celebrate with crackers and lion dances, which is what we used to do in Vietnam. Here we have a party, music, a band or the cinema.

In Vietnam, people buy those little bushes with tiny 'oranges' for New Year -- what are they called?

It's the kumquat tree and the mai flower which blossoms only at Tet.

And now your life is in England thousands of miles away, do you accept it?

Compared with millions of people still in Vietnam, with people in the Sudan, in Ethiopia, and so on, we are very lucky. Compared with Cambodia!

Also Vietnamese people are very strong. They are survivors.

Yes, we've had war constantly. Occupied by the Chinese for a thousand years, then by the French. We have had to be strong mentally to survive. In the end, if you want to have a better life, you have to work hard. I always tell my children that. If they want to live comfortably they have to study and find a job. I tell the other Vietnamese in Bristol that they cannot sit around and moan about the weather -- there are millions in Vietnam suffering. Here you have to go out and study English, find a hobby, or support a football team as I do -- Liverpool! But the Vietnamese are survivors -- the percentage of suicides among South East Asian people is much lower than among Europeans, even though we are poorer.

You must miss the emotional as well as the physical landscape, not only the beauty of Vietnam, but the spirit of its people.

Yes, it's very hard. So most people want to go back for a holiday at least ... I have been to America six times, and I have been to France nine times, but I still prefer to go back to Vietnam -- I feel very attached to my country. My brother and family who live in America are surprised that I go back, they think there is nothing to see but poverty, corruption, oppression; they say I should go and see the Niagara Falls or go to Brazil or even China ... but I want to go back -- just to go back to my home ... that's all.

[Interview with **Geraldine Edwards**]

Mai Van Thong was born in 1939 in Hanoi, Vietnam and qualified as a pharmacist in 1959. Since 1983 he has been working as the Project Co-ordinator for the Vietnamese Community in the Bristol and District area. He has a son and daughter. His interests include football, tennis, cinema, music and reading.

Thưa anh, mỗi người có một chuyện khác nhau. Xin anh cho biết tới nước Anh khi nào, đã ở đây được 14 năm chưa và tới nước Anh như thế nào?

Tôi tới nước Anh vào tháng năm 1979. Gia đình tôi được tàu Anh cứa và được đưa tới Hồng Kông. Sau ba tuần, máy bay chở chúng tôi sang nước Anh. Chúng tôi ở tại trung tâm tiếp cứ gần Christchurch, Bournemouth và ở đó được khoảng bốn tháng rưỡi thì được cho nhà ở tỉnh Bath và sống từ đó đến giờ.

Anh ở trên thuyền được bao nhiêu lâu? Anh có sợ không?

Gia đình tôi ở trên thuyền được hai ngày rưỡi. Tôi không thấy sợ vì ở tầng dưới nên không nhìn thấy gì cả. Thuyền thì quá nhỏ, dài có 25 mét, rộng 5 mét mà chứa tới 605 người. Tôi đi với vợ và hai con.

Tôi nhớ là anh nói là tình cờ mà anh tới nước Anh vì được tàu Anh cứu. Còn những thân quyến khác của anh thì được tàu Pháp và Mỹ cứu hay sao?

Sáu anh chị em tôi chạy thoát vào 1975 khi mọi người thi nhau chạy ra ngoại quốc. Ba người được Pháp nhận, ba người được Mỹ nhận, vì vậy, ba anh em ở Pháp và ba anh em ở Mỹ. Riêng tôi, tôi không ân hận gì cả vì tin vào số mệnh. Đời sống ở bên Anh chậm hơn các nước khác ví dụ Mỹ. ở nước Anh khó mà làm giầu nhưng ít ra còn có nhiều thời giờ để nghỉ ngơi. Mọi người ít phải tranh đua với cuộc sống nên con người không trở

nên ích kỷ, tàn nhẫn như ở Mỹ vì phải chạy theo đồng tiền nên con người dễ trở nên bần tiện.

Thế bây giờ anh ở nước Anh. Anh còn nhớ cảm tưởng đầu tiên khi tới nước Anh không?

Cảm tưởng đầu tiên của tôi khi tới nước Anh là khi được xe chở từ phi trường Heathrow tới trung tâm tiếp cư Sopley và dọc đường xe dừng lại ở vài nơi giải khát. Tôi nhìn xung quanh...... Thời tiết còn lạnh mà chúng tôi lại không có đủ quần áo ấm. Khi lên máy bay, chúng tôi không có gì cả. Vài người còn không có giầy mà đi. Ở trên thuyền thì thở không nổi vì vừa hấp hơi vừa nóng nên mọi người phải cởi bớt quần áo. Khi được tàu Anh cứu, tôi nhìn quanh tôi nhưng không thấy quần áo đâu nữa cho nên khi trèo thang giây lên tàu Anh thì thấy mình chỉ mặc có áo may ô và quần đùi còn mọi thứ thì mất hết. Mọi người đều đồng cảnh ngộ và đều hy vọng tàu Anh sẽ cung cấp cho mọi thứ nhưng vì tàu là tàu thương mại, chở đồ từ Ấn độ sang nước Anh. Họ đâu có ngờ là sẽ cứu người ngoài biên, vì vậy, họ không có đồ ăn cho chúng tôi. Họ cứu chúng tôi vừa là tình cờ mà gặp vừa là nhân đạo. Họ cho chúng tôi những gì mà họ có. Họ không cứa một thuyền mà cứu thêm một thuyền khác nữa, vì vậy có hơn ngàn người trên tàu. Chúng tôi, dù sao, cũng may mắn là còn có được chút ít và ăn. Chúng tôi ngủ trên boong tàu và ở trên, tàu được bốn ngày thì tàu tới Hồng Kông. Sau đó vài ngày thì tàu được cập bến và chúng tôi được đưa vào một trại giam bởi vì chúng tôi được tàu Anh cứu (khác với những người không được tàu Anh cứu thì đưa vào trại tỵ nạn). Chúng tôi ở đó 3 tuần và không được đi ra ngoài. Họ không đưa tất cả mọi người sang nước Anh một lúc mà đưa từ từ và gia đình tôi rời gần chót. Gia đình tôi luôn sống bên nhau. Hai con tôi một 6 tuổi, một 7 tuổi – Chúng biết hết mọi chuyện sẩy ra và con gái tôi có viết lại chuyện vượt biển vài năm sau.

Anh đã về Việt Nam lại chưa?

Tôi về Việt Nam hai lần vào 1993 và 1995. Tôi về với gia đình. Tôi chỉ còn đẳng vợ ở đó và tôi rất xúc động khi nhìn lại quê hương. Tôi rất quyến luyến với quê hương. Tôi đã ở trong quân đội, đã đổ mồ hôi xương máu cho đất nước. Vì thua trận nên chúng tôi phải sống lưu vong ở nước Anh. Đối với những người nghèo ở Việt Nam thì nước Anh là thiên đường. Nhưng đối với tôi thì khác vì tôi có một mức sống dễ dàng ở Việt Nam. Tôi là dược sĩ, có mở dược phòng nên đời sống thải mái. Nhưng tới nước Anh tôi nghĩ mức sống của tôi bị giảm xuống nhiều, ngược lại đối với những người nghèo ở Việt Nam thì lại tăng.

Bây giờ sống ở Tây phương, anh nghĩ thế vào về các báo cáo của báo chí, truyền thanh, truyền hình về cuộc chiến tranh ở Việt Nam? Tôi nghĩ là anh không bao giờ có được một quan điểm chính xác về chiến cuộc đó.

Báo chí, truyền thanh, truyền hình đã đối xử rất là bất công đối với miền Nam. Họ chiếu trên Ti Vi những độc ác của quân đội miền Nam, của quân đội Mỹ nhưng họ không bao giờ chiếu sự tàn bạo của quân Cộng Sản. Thật là bất công! Tôi lên án

phong trào phản chiến ở nước Anh, nước Mỹ. Tôi lên án báo chí, John Lennon, Jane Fonda, Joan Baed ...... Họ thật là ngu xuẩn. Tôi nhớ John Lennon và Yoko Ono đã như trần trồng cho báo chí chụp hình để phản đối chiến tranh Việt Nam. Họ đã làm hại miền Nam vì họ không hiểu biết gì về chiến trạnh này. Họ không biết tới những cực khổ khi bị giam ở các trại cải tạo mà tôi đã bị gần 3 năm.

Trước khi miền Nam sụp đổ, dân chúng ở trên thế giới vì không hiểu Cộng sản nên phần đông đã ưng hộ Cộng sản. Sau khi miền Nam sụa đổ, họ thấy triệu triệu người miền Nam đã liều mạng vượt biển ra đi. Lúc đo, họ mới bắt đầu hiểu chế độ Cộng sản là như thế nào thì đã muộn rồi. Tôi bị tống vào trai cải tạo. Điều đáng sợ nhất là Cộng sản không tuyên án, vì vậy, không biết bao giờ được thả. Họ chỉ nói là khi nào nhà nước thấy là đáng được thả thì họ sẽ thả còn nếu không thì tù mọt gông. Ngay cả khi được thả rồi, cải tạo viên cũng thành vô tích sự vì không có cơ quan nào mướn họ. Hiện nay thì chính phủ Việt Nam đã mở rộng chính sách phần nào.

Nhiều người miền Nam là dân trí thức. Tôi nhớ là đã nói chuyện với nhiều phu xe xích lô là giáo sư dạy toán, dạy Anh văn trước khi bị đi cải tạo.

Khi tôi về Việt Nam tôi di chuyển bằng xích lô và có nói chuyện với họ. Phần đông không phải dân quê mà là dân có học hoặc sĩ quan quân đội miền Nam. Họ vẫn giữ được phẩm cách và rất tự ái. Tôi có trả thêm tiền nhưng họ không bao gio lấy. Họ biết kiếm tiền ở ngoại quốc rất là gay go. Chỉ có những người ít học mới nghĩ là kiếm tiền dễ dàng ở ngoại quốc, còn người có học biết là kiếm tiền rất khó ở nước ngoài.

Có vài người đã về sống lại ở Việt Nam. Điều này có khó khăn cho những người như anh không?

Hiện giờ chính phủ Việt Nam chỉ cho về ở lại những người trên 60 tuổi. Nhưng những người ở các trại ở Hồng Kồng thi bị cưỡng bách hồi hương bởi vì họ không phải là ty nạn chính trị và là ty nạn kinh tế, vì vậy không nước nào nhận họ và họ bị trục xuất về. Chính phủ Việt Nam ngày trước đã không dùng dân trí thức, sau này thì đã dùng bởi yì nhận thức được sự quan trọng của "chất sám" vì não bộ điều động cơ thể chư không phải bắp thịt. Nếu chính phư cứ tiếp tục dùng ngưới ngu dốt để điều hành đất nước như những năm trước đây thì nước Việt Nam sẽ thụt luì. Bây giờ thì chính phủ đã nhận biết là không thể chỉ dùng các đảng viên mà phải dùng dân trí thức và khoa học kỹ thuật. Trước đây, chính phủ không dùng dân trí thức bởi vì thành phần này hay thắc mắc mà chỉ dùng đảng viên là các người cuồng tín. Những người này thi hành mệnh lệnh như cái máy và không đặt câu hơi như những người có học? Cũng may chính phủ đã mở mắt và dùng lại người có học. Kể ra hơi muộn nhưng vẫn còn hơn. Tôi nghĩ là Việt Nam chậm tiến khoảng 30 năm so với Thái Lan và Mã Lai, khoảng 50 năm so với nước Anh nhưng Việt Nam sẽ bắt kip vì dân Việt Nam thông minh và chịu khó. Hãy nhìn gia đình tôi làm ví dụ. Lúc mới định cư ở nước Anh, gia đình tôi tay trắng. Hiện giơ tất cả gia đính tôi đều đi làm, vợ tôi làm cho hãng điện tử Horstman, con trai tôi tập sự bác si và số dân Việt Nam thất nghiệp ở Avon chỉ có 6%.

Có ít người Việt ở Bristol. Họ có thấy lẻ loi không?

Có khoảng 360 người Việt ở Bristol. Trừ những người nhiều tuổi thì phần đông đều làm việc vất vả nên không thấy lẻ loi. Như tôi chẳng han đi làm tư thứ hai đến thứ sáu. Thứ bảy đi sắm đồ với vợ. Chủ nhật coi đá banh trên Ti Vi nên không thấy buồn. Tôi nghĩ có lẽ nên có những cộng đồng nhơ hơn là những cộng đồng lớn bơi vì tỉ lệ dân Việt Nam thất nghiệp ở Luân dôn là 60%. Điều này cũng dễ hiểu bởi vì sống ở tỉnh nhơ mà thất nghiệp thi buồn và mặc cảm còn sống ở tỉnh lớn có nhiều người thất nghiệp thì không cảm thấy như vậy mặc dầu họ biết là gánh nặng cho xã hội. Hàng ngày, họ thấy những người xung quanh cũng đồng cảnh ngộ nên họ không thấy đơn độc nhưng dần dần họ mất hết sự hăng hái đi tìm việc làm, vì vậy, nói là vấn đề nào cũng có bề phải, bề trái là cũng đúng vậy.

Chắc anh nhớ đồ àn Việt Nam? Anh làm thế nào để thay thế?

Tôi dùng đồ ăn Trung Quốc để thay thế.

Tôi rất quan tâm khi anh nói anh theo đạo Phật. Ở Bristol có ngôi chùa nào không?

Tôi mộ đạo Phật Nhưng chỉ Luân dôn mới có chùa chứ ở Bath và Bristol thì không. Tôi có nhận được sách báo, kinh phật của chùa Luân dôn. Tôi tin tưởng vào đức Phật, con trai tôi cũng vậy. Con gái tôi không biết sao. Vợ tôi có bàn thờ Phật nhưng không mộ đạo Phật như tôi. Con tôi sang Thái Lan sống trong chùa 10 ngày như một ông sư.

Con của anh bây giờ nghĩ mình là người Việt hay là người Anh? Bởi vì chúng sinh đẻ ở Việt Nam và tới nước Anh khi còn nhơ, anh có nghĩ là có sư xung đột về tư tưởng khi vừa là người Anh vừa là người Việt không?

Các con tôi là người Việt nhưng sự suy nghĩ của chúng thì 90% là người Anh. Tất nhiên có sự xung đột giữa hai nền văn hóa nhưng chúng cũng biết cái nào sai, cái nào đúng. Khi các con tôi về Việt Nam chơi, chúng cư xử như người Việt Nam nhưng khi về lại nước Anh, chúng trở thành người Anh. Tuy nhiên, chúng luôn luôn kinh nể và vâng lời cha mẹ.

Giữa người Việt và người Anh, giữa phương Tây và phương Đông, có một đường lối suy nghĩ và một triết lý về đới sống khác nhau. người Việt cơ vẻ rất thản nhiên về đơi sống và chấp nhận số mệnh.....

Các con tôi có lẽ suy nghĩ như người Anh nhưng chúng vẫn là người Việt. Tôi có nói với các con tôi là phải gìn giữ văn hóa Việt Nam vì có nhiều điều tốt, ví dụ như vâng lới cha me, thờ kính tổ tiên và đùm bọc lẫn nhau. Cha mẹ không phải là ban mà là cố vấn. Ở nước Anh, con cái nghĩ cha mẹ là ban, có điều là khi cha mẹ già, họ lại để cha mẹ vào nhà dưỡng lão. Đối với người Việt thi là độc ác!

Những người nhiều tuổi ở Việt Nam được kính trọng và coi là cố vấn. Ở nước Anh ít thấy đông người già ngoài đường. Ở Việt Nam trái lại vào 6 giờ sáng, các đường phố và công viên đầy người già đi bộ, chạy bộ, tập thể thao, tập võ và họ thường đi ra ngoài vào buổi tối. Thật khó cho người già Việt Nam sống ở nước Anh......

Đúng, thật là khó. Nhiều người rất lẻ loi vì khí hậu, trở ngại ngôn ngữ. Trước dây, tôi có tở chức cơm trưa cho họ.

Thế còn Tết Việt Nam? Dân Việt Nam có liên hoan Tết ở nước Anh hay không? Ở Việt Nam thật là

vui với pháo nổ như bom!

Có, chúng tôi có tổ chức Tết ở nước Anh. Ở Việt Nam vài năm sau này cấm đốt pháo. Mọi người đều bất bình vì Tết không có pháo không phải là Tết!

Tại sao lại cấm đốt pháo – có phải vì pháo nguy hiểm không?

Không – Chính phư nói là tốn tiền vô ích!

Người dân cần phải được liên hoan Tết và đốt pháo.

Đúng vây. Pháo là để đuổi ma, đuổi quỉ, đuổi mọi sự xui xẻo trong năm qua và đón mọi sự may mắn trong năm tới vì vây, pháo gắn liền với Tết. Tết Việt Nam chùng với Tết Trung quốc và được liên hoa với pháo và múa lân. Ở đây vì vấn đề tài chánh và địa điểm, hội Việt Nam tổ chức tiện liên hoan và chiếu bóng.

Ở Việt Nam, người dân mua những cây nho nhỏ có trái nhơ mà vàng cam vào dịa Tết.

Đó la cây quất mà trái gọi là trái quất hay trái tắc và người ta cũng trưng hoa mai màu vàng vào Tết.

Bây giờ anh sống ở Bath, ở nước Anh xa Việt Nam ngàn trùng..... Anh có chấp nhận không?

Tôi vẫn nghĩ là so sánh với triệu triệu người ở Việt Nam, ở Sudan, Ethiopia.... tôi thât là hết sức may mắn.

Người Việt Nam rất là mạnh mẽ về tinh thần. Họ luôn luôn phấn đấu và sống sót.

Đúng vậy, Việt Nam luôn luôn có chiến tranh. Bị đô hô bởi Trung Quốc một ngàn năm rồi bị nguoi Phạp xâm chiếm. Nếu chiếm. Nếu ngưới Việt không mạnh về tinh thần thi không sống sót nổi. Nói chung, nếu muốn có một đời sống tốt đẹp hơn thì phải chịu khó làm việc, điều này tôi luôn luôn căn dặn các con tôi. Nếu muốn sống thoải mái thì phải chịu khó học hành để có một nghề. Tôi cũng có nói với những Việt khác ở Bristol là không thể ngồi một chỗ và than thở về thời tiết ..... Hãy đi học Anh văn, tìm một thú tiêu khiển như xem đá banh và ủng hộ một đội banh (như tôi chẳng hạn, ủng hộ Liverpool) cho thêm phần hào hứng. Dù thế nào chăng nữa, dân Việt Nam vẫn sống còn, bằng cớ tỉ lệ dân Á Châu tự tử rất là thấp so với Âu Châu dù là nghèo hơn.

Có một cái gì rất đặc biệt về Việt Nam, không phải chỉ là vẻ đẹp của quê hương mà là tinh thần dân tộc. Chắc anh nhớ cả hai điều trên....

Đúng vậy! Không thể nào quên được, vì vậy, phần đông dân Việt Nam đều muốn về thăm quê hương. Tôi đã sang Mỹ 6 lần, sang Pháp 9 lần nhưng tôi vẫn thấy thích về Việt Nam hơn bởi vì tôi rất quyến luyến quê hương tôi. Anh chị em tôi và bạn bè rất ngạc nhiên vì họ nghĩ có gì mà xem ở Việt Nam ngoài nghèo khổ, tham nhũng và áp bức. Họ nói tôi nên đi nghỉ hè ở Canada, đi xem thác Niagara, đi Brazil hoặc Trung Quốc.... Nhưng họ nói mặc họ nói, tôi vẫn muốn về thăm Việt Nam, quê hương bất diệt của tôi.

1976

Mammy and Daddy told us we were leaving. I firstly imagined we would load all our possessions on the back of a flat cart drawn, perhaps, by a gently plodding horse; or a big old truck with enormous black wheels you could stand on. I thought we would gracefully pull out of the village, sitting among our possessions, as the settlers I had seen on the telly.

With difficulty I tried to accept that not only would I have to leave our house, where we had had so many fights, laughs, good food and growing pains; but would also have to say goodbye to a kaleidoscope of childhood memories. Special private places enjoyed on warm summer afternoons -- or crisp autumnal mornings walking on the strand, when the tide stretched thin and small in the distance, over the wrinkled sand at low tide, when everything smelled so fresh, clean and exhilarating. A rich tapestry of excitement, familiarity, beauty and fun.

My illusions were further clouded when I realised that we were not staying in Ireland but moving to England. My idea of England was confused. Not only was it the destructive, brooding tyrant of current news, history books and songs, but also the place where my mother spent her childhood. Her father, my grandfather, was English. Her mother had moved to pre-war England from a village two miles up the coast from ours. When my mother was fifteen their family had moved back to Ireland, settling in the village to run a 'bed and breakfast' at the idyllic seaside.

Mammy told me that when they first came to Ireland in 1950, she was amazed that you could walk into a shop and buy as much food as you had money for, without a ration book. There was food everywhere, or at least it must have seemed so after London, where food was scarce, still heavily rationed and the skyline and people broken and scarred after the wreckage of the war. Ireland, to her delight, was the land not only of milk and honey, but suffused too with the delicious aroma of bacon and eggs, roast dinners and other culinary enchantments.

People always went overseas. As new generations were born, other countries seized their share of fresh talent and energy. Myriads disappeared into this labyrinth of cities to work and live. If they did return, they came disguised in a veneer of others, their voices different, airs and graces assumed as one who was well travelled, had seen the world and now realised that the beauty of our special place was not so great after all. They returned as holiday-makers, briefly in the warm sun, to play on the beach and watch with detached envy the fishermen unloading their catch onto the quay. Then they were gone, summer romance ended, and winter held the village in a quiet time of dark evenings, autumnal colours fading into the cool blue and grey of stormy skies. When the wind roared high in the trees and all around the cliffs, battering the sea into tremendous ephemeral sculptures, running along the wide strand, I was wild and free in the special emptiness of winter. I mourned the fact that we would leave before I could do this again, when the trees were just starting to glow and burn with the glory of autumn.

My father had been offered work in England, my mother told us, keeping from us the economic realities of rural living. The images of England I had formed in my mind were then a strange mixture: one reflected its nickname, The Black Country -- heavy industry, few fields of grass, where food was scarce, rationed and unappealing, a culinary desert, where children didn't know where milk

I shall not hit boys over the head
even when they have been racist
bullies

came from. Imagine that! Other images, collected from films I had seen and stories Mammy had told us, swam around my vivid imagination: of London during the war, sailing boats, sepia round-edged photographs of long-skirted women and stiff-necked moustachioed men.

I imagined my father leaving our small English house, standing on the pavement by the front door, saying, 'I'm off down t'pit' in his rapidly assimilated and mandatory new accent. He would then walk up the street, packed tight with other houses all the same, up the steep hill, sunshine glinting on the rain-wet cobbles. He would naturally have to wear a lean black suit, with narrow collar and flat cap, metal 'snap' box tucked under his arm, on his way with t'other men. Mammy would stand at the door, flower-sprigged house coat on, waving goodbye, her curlered hair contained by a solid scarf. I conveniently overlooked that my mother had short hair and that my father was a builder and carpenter.

We sold and gave away most of the detritus a large family collects; it was a strange, sad and exciting process. Saying goodbye to our friends and relations was impossibly hard. I tried to laugh it off, disguising my confusion and grief with the moody, withdrawn behaviour of adolescence.

Woken in darkness, we rushed around, grabbing the last of the feel of the house, hushed, excited and anxious. As the cars pulled out of the village I looked back. In the dim light of dawn a figure stood, silent, huddled against the raw cold of the hour, watching us go. As we drove towards the ferry on that exquisite September morning, light misted and glowed softly, rolling over the slope of the hills and around the trees. A rabbit, confused and frantic, skitted and zigzagged across the road in front of us, crunching under the wheels and flipping to the roadside, torn, flattened and bloody. My eyes fixed on the poor limp blob until we rounded the bend. I allowed myself to cry for the rabbit.

The ferry was an amazing place, much bigger than anything on earth. We watched nervously, in awe of the other passengers and crew; of everything. Pressing our faces through the heavy metal gates which divided first from second class, containing us -- as I had seen in a film about the Titanic, all the poor Irish people in third class were locked in the lower decks and died screaming and praying. I concentrated on our exploration of the ship. We climbed to the highest point, overshadowed by the towering funnel, and sat for most of the journey, free and windblown. We watched Ireland recede into a diminishing thin line, framed by the widening furrow of white water behind us.

We were foot passengers and would travel on from Fishguard by train. We carried some luggage in bags Mammy had bought in Wexford. My bag had 'Arsenal the Gunners' printed on one side. Overly nervous of our likely reception in England, an Irish family with 'The Gunners' as an emblem, my mother instructed me to scrub out the G and paint in a more innocuous R. 'The Runners' sounded stupid, I thought -- all footballers should at least be able to run. My bag held an odd assortment of treasured possessions -- a few books and smooth, rounded pebbles and a peacock feather, its beauty crushed and diminished by the addition of some clothes. Large wooden crates accompanied us as freight; it was strange to see our lives compacted into square boxes.

I felt I was already a different person by the time we arrived in Fishguard. Standing on the platform which curved into the distance, I felt small. Strong wafts of fumes and sounds echoed and distorted into the high ceiling. I had never been on a train before and was anxious not to betray my lack of experience. I strained to assume a nonchalant poise, doubtless producing a bizarre sequence of facial contortions.

London's hulking, noisy mass absorbed us, lost in the screams of the rush hour, assailed by a baffling mix of sights, smells and sounds; strange sharp, high voices echoed across the evening. The city was alive, an enormous creature, devouring all. Through the flesh of this lumbering animal we went and were spat out the other side, towards Norwich. Then, seasoned traveller that I was now, having been engaged in this most mind-expanding pursuit for almost 15 hours, I allowed myself to stop gaping at everything in this most strange of countries and slipped into the familiar, cosy darkness of sleep.

Norwich exploded into a hectic rush of orange light as we arrived, sleepy and irritably cold late that night. Everything, the tall buildings, the sky and the myriads of traffic glared orange. The stars were lost in the fog of the city's glow. Where had my beautiful black velvet sky gone? The cathedral, bathed in beams of strong light, held my attention briefly, my face pressed to the window of the taxi, trying to make some sense of this strange place.

Our new home was small, joined to the others as in my fantasy, in a long, winding street. Red brick formed every wall and I was fascinated by the texture and warm glow of the colour. Fascination mixed with fear. Familiarity with a small village was no preparation for thousands of streets and millions of houses, all the same. I was gripped by anxiety, terrified that I would lose myself in this Hitchcockian dream-scape maze of buildings and streets. There was no familiar rugged coastline and great expanse of sea, no empty fields with the church spire standing slender and sure. I kept my solitary exploration to the tiny garden and the small corner shop.

We continued with the long processes of acclimatisation. The city and its shops astounded us. 'Anglia Square', a monstrosity of late-sixties urban development, a tatty shopping arcade with its concentration of shops, lured and dazzled us.

My first taste of English food brought a wave of consternation. I prayed that this disgusting taste and consistency was limited to 'Shredded Wheat', or else I would have to leave. But the supermarkets reassured me -- Aladdin's caves full of wonderful things to eat. I marvelled at the selection of food, not at all like my mental picture of the culinary desert.

We were dispatched to various schools according to our respective ages. I was to attend the local comprehensive school, an enormous vaulted Victorian building which smelled musty and strange. One thousand pupils went there. Fear gripped my stomach at the thought of such numbers. The National (primary) School in the village back home had under one hundred pupils and only three nun teachers. There were 500 pupils on the Lower site where I would start, and I walked terrified, lonely and painfully awkward to meet my fate. I tried to imagine so many people together in one place.

What if I was beaten up? I had heard of terrible fights and bullying in English schools. Someone in the newspapers had said that schools were full of anger, frustration and unhappiness. I expected the worst.

I wasn't beaten up -- not physically, anyway. I was continually assailed by rabid groups of power-hungry adolescents for the first few weeks and on through the years, their taunts eventually becoming worn custom, a familiar greeting. They shouted, 'Hey, Irish Paddy, say it. Go on, say Tirty tree and a turd. Top of the morning to ya. Begorra.' This sort of thing kept them amused for hours. I also painfully learned how childish it was to call my parents Mammy and Daddy and rapidly assumed the foreign Mum and Dad into my vocabulary.

The more they assailed, criticised and laughed at me, the more my pride grew, fierce and strong. One particular incident of spiteful bullying seemed to turn the tide in my favour.

One boy in my class -- an immature, intensely irrating and spotty little creep -- by way of habit entertained himself and his mates by calling me the usual range of names and insults, accusing me of planting bombs. This was in the confined, anarchic and potentially explosive period before the teacher had entered the class at the beginning of a lesson. He always called me a 'T'ick Oirish Paddy'. He continued his taunts long after the others had tired, until my remote composure finally snapped and I exploded on him, unleashing pent-up frustration and anger. I lunged at him, beating him repeatedly with the only weapon to hand -- my gym shoes -- just as the teacher walked into the room behind me.

She stood watching me exact my revenge. The class were transfixed, time-frozen. She was an older woman, nearing retirement, very fusty and given to fits of apoplexy and hyper-tension when disciplining wayward pupils. She exploded, arching her powerful voice high into the ceiling and right through my bones, immediately freezing me, plimsoll poised above the worm's cowering head.

I was charged, convicted and sentenced before you could blink an eye. For my crime of unprovoked assault I was sentenced to 1,000 lines. She wouldn't hear my protests, lashing out in anger that her class had been disrupted. She failed, however, to give me an actual line. When I tried to point this out to her, she didn't want to hear another word. I suffered the ignominy in silence, secretly completing my barbed punishment at home to present to her on Monday. I created my own line: 'I shall not hit boys over the head, even when they have been racist bullies.'

Bristling with pride, I presented her with exactly 1,000 lines on Monday morning, hoping to score my point, for her to realise how wrong she had been, that I was an innocent, wrongly treated, that I deserved respect and vindication. Wrong! She glanced at me with a remote expression on her face. She had forgotten. She just didn't remember the mortifying trial, conviction and sentence. She glanced hastily over the copious sheets of paper, not even reading them, and brushed me away, talking with another teacher. I was dismissed, irrelevant. She didn't care. Having inflicted a puerile, boring and totally ineffective form of discipline on me, she swept me aside as she would an irritating fly.

At least my persecutors realised that I was not as passive as my glazed exterior suggested, my composure was capable of cracking. I realised, too, that it was possible to seek revenge and halt the continual onslaught, for a while at least.

For months, though, I still wallowed in self pity, aching for the sea and space of Ireland. I hated the bleak flatness of Norfolk with an almost consuming force, despising the pathetic cluttered, shabby and vandalised parks where we went to get some air. In Ireland we had space, millions of it, in the house, countryside and sea. In Norwich we were confined, caged and confused. I pined for the cliffs, bays, beach, rock pools and the majestic, powerfully alive water. I hated the barren and boring coastline of Norfolk and despised the soft rolling flatness of the land. I hated this place with an implacable stubborness of one who will not open her eyes to see.

Eventually, a thaw began to warm my feelings towards our new home. I started, halting and afraid, to develop friendships at school. A group of girls allowed me to tag along, I suspect for the novelty aspect. They initiated me into the many secrets of teenage existence. As we grew together, the bitchiness receded and I found a friendship which was warm and exciting.

I was changing, assimilating the culture of this foreign land. I knew that when we returned to Ireland, it would be as different people. From the first time I set foot in England, I never felt I really belonged. Once we left, I felt I couldn't belong in Ireland any more, either. I had joined the ranks of the displaced. Like thousands of others, I struggle to find my place.

Trish McGrath is 34, lives in Easton, Bristol and works as a freelance community arts worker. She is completing her first novel.

MOHAMMED SYEED

My Sister Garsera

When I was seven, I used to live in Somalia. I lived with my sister, Garsera. She is married and has five children. She always made me stay in the house. One day I had a fight with my sister. She hit me and did not give me any food. Then I went out and got some sweet potatoes and gave them to her. Then she was happy.

Another day I ran away from Garsera's house and went to my other sister. Her name is Shukri and she lived in a town called Soka. She sold potatoes and other vegetables. She was alright with me and never hit me. When I went to her house, she asked, 'why have you come here? Do you want something?' I said, 'yes, please. Can I have some sweet potatoes for my sister, Garsera?'

Shukri gave me some potatoes. Then I went back to Garsera's house. When I went inside, Garsera was very angry with me, but when I gave her the potatoes she was happy. Then she gave me some food.

Another day I went to my sister, Shukri's house again. As I was walking along the road I found some money. I bought some sweets and many other things with the money. I hired a bicycle and went out riding on it.

After a week, the money had all gone. Then I started stealing money from my sister Garsera. She kept her money in a secret box. It had numbers on it. I had seen her open the box, and I remembered the numbers. So when my sister went out to the doctor, I opened the box and took some money. I used to take money every day from different places where she kept it.

One day she found out. She saw a pen which I had bought with the money. She asked, 'where did you get the money for this pen?' I said, 'a boy in the school broke my new pencil that you bought me. So the teacher gave me

this pen.' Then Garsera came to the school to check if I was telling the truth. She asked the teacher if she had given the pen to me. The teacher, of course, said no. Then Garsera grabbed my arm and dragged me to her house. She said, 'wait here', and went to check the money in her box. I knew I was in big trouble, so I ran away.

I went to my other sister's house. I said to her, 'Garsera wants two hundred pounds. She needs the money to take her baby to the doctor.' I was lying. But she believed me and gave me the money.

I took the money and ran away. I was walking along a road and saw a lot of trucks going by. I asked one truck driver for a lift. He asked, 'where do you want to go?' I said I was trying to go to the town of Arab sea. The driver said, 'oh, you are lucky because I am going to Arab sea but you will have to climb on to the back of the truck.'

The truck was loaded with vegetables. I climbed up on top of some bags of vegetables. It took me five days to get to this town. There, I met my cousin, Fatima. She had a house, and used to sell vegetables on the street. I stayed with her for five days. I played with a boy who lived next door called Abdi. One night I had a fight with him and beat him up. His mother complained to my cousin, who said, 'go back to your sister.'

Instead I took a bus and went to Ethiopia. I got off the bus in the middle of the road, it was too far from the town. The people there spoke both Somali and Ethiopian. They had many animals, camels, sheep, cows and horses. A man asked where I came from, and I said from Soka.

He asked, 'where are you going?' I said to another town called Allaibari. He said, 'oh, that's too far, it will take you about five days to walk there.' I said, 'I must go there.' He said, 'people try to walk there and they are eaten by wild animals. You can stay with us as long as you like.' I stayed with them just for one night. In the morning, I left, saying 'I like your house, but I must go home.' I tried to walk to Allaibari. I had to go through a jungle, but there were no people there. I was a bit scared because in that jungle there were foxes and wild cats. I started running and went back to Soka.

Then I went back to my sister, Garsera. She was very worried about me and when I came back she gave me some food and was very nice to me. Garsera's husband was on holiday from Saudi Arabia. He gave me a lot of money and I tried to run away again.

I went to my mum's house in the countryside. As I came near, I felt very tired and hungry. I saw lots of fruit on trees and picked some. I was worried that somebody might catch me picking the fruit, but later I found the fruit trees belonged to my mother.

A few days later, Garsera came to the house. She was worried about me, but was happy when she saw me there. She wanted to take me back to her home, but I did not want to go. My other sister, Sophia, came to my mum's house as well. She asked, 'do you want to go to England?' I said yes please, and so she took me to Ethiopia.

I have another sister called Rosina, who lives in London. Her husband came to Ethiopia to take me and my little nephew to London. My sister said, 'you have to go dressed as a girl.' I was shocked to hear this, but agreed when she showed me the papers and explained the situation. Then she said, 'you must practise acting like a girl.'

When I went out dressed like a girl, all the people were looking at me. I had a girl's dress, lipstick and some black stuff on my eyes. I had high heel shoes, so I could not walk very well. I kept falling down. When I was walking near my house people thought I was a girl. They did not recognise me. I had to dress up like a girl because I used the papers of my sister, Hafia. They did not let her come because she was too old, she was twenty-two.

When we came to the airport in Ethiopia I was really worried. I thought the people there might find out that I was not a girl. They searched me with a metal detector. I had a pen in my pocket and the machine started making a noise. I was really scared but in the end they let me go.

We got on the aeroplane and after seven hours we came to London airport. Some women took me to a room to check me. I was worried because in the room some women had to take their clothes off. I felt very embarrassed as well. Luckily, I did not have to undress. Then I came out and waited for my brother-in-law.

After half an hour he arrived and asked an officer, 'where is my daughter?' The officer replied, 'she is sitting there waiting for you,' and I had to pretend to be his daughter.

Then we left the airport. My sister could not recognise me. When my brother-in-law told them that I was dressed as a girl, they all started to laugh. I did not like it and I got a bit cross. I had two apples under my jumper to make me look like a girl. So I took them out and started to eat them. That is how I came to Bristol.

Round Barrows in a Rapefield

Two myrtle mounds wait to pounce
in a sudden sea of chrome
crouch cat-like in the oilseed
to guard the once sacred land
iron bones fashioned from ochre burnt
returned to ancestral loam

the citrous acre sings out
unashamed as a suburban parlour
in the midday sun

yellow is our rape of the earth
and Vincent's last blazing look at a cornfield world
against the black, fleeing crows
over the mendip horizon a viridian fringe of trees
swish like a crematorium backdrop

only a week later
cut down by the lammas scythe
my mother's dead jaw hangs slack
in a green/yellow field of a face
far from where the Russian steppes of her birthland
billow with golden wheat

now, olev ha shalom,
both parents lie scattered husks on a foreign soil
while its original occupants
are plastered over with margerine
yitgadahl v'yitkaddash shmey rabah
for all our ancestors
sing unashamedly yellow in the midday sun!

Rachael Clyne is a psychotherapist whose parents were Russian. She is now studying for a fine art degree at the University of the West of England.

MARGARET GRIEW

Family Ghosts

I have always felt an affinity with things Russian: the deep, expansive novels of Dostoyevsky and Tolstoy, and the vast landscapes described by Pasternak, all long ago caught in my imagination. It is no wonder, for my origins are behind what used to be the Iron Curtain. Until lately, this fact aroused feelings of conflict in me. The need we all have for seeking out our roots was tempered by my abhorrence of the communist system, for I have read the searing accounts of dissidents such as Solzhenitsyn and Bukovsky, and one cannot ignore the plight of the refuseniks.

But now eastern Europe has opened up and recently, while watching television, I found the urge to know more about my antecedents was reawakened. There, on the screen in my living room, I thought I saw my long-dead grandfather. He was one of the stocky Poles at a Solidarity meeting, sporting the same clipped toothbrush moustache that I knew as a child. He had been a quiet, serious man of whom I was somewhat in awe -- perhaps it was the prickly kiss that disturbed me -- although I knew him to be kind and caring.

He had come to this country as a small child from Poland, with his family, towards the end of the last century. The Jews of Cracow were renowned for their learning. My great-grandfather Aaron had been no exception and had spent his life studying in that ancient university town of Bohemia. He was asthmatic and without a proper trade and wished to escape the possibility of pogroms and conscription. It was, in fact, my grandfather who became the family breadwinner in London, making fur muffs at the age of thirteen. He worked hard and late in the sweatshop and was often found by his mother asleep on the stairs at night, fully clothed. This hard work paid off: he later owned a prosperous furrier business and I remember as a small child proudly wearing a white fur coat and hat which set off my shiny dark ringlets marvellously.

Grandpa Maurice wanted to marry my great-aunt Louisa, a fun-loving, histrionic lady (an actress manquée, just as my vivacious sister was later to be), but she wouldn't have him. She and her family also came from Cracow but were, by then, a jolly, anglicised lot. Her sister, Katie, made grandpa a perfect wife instead and we all loved her.

As I write, more family ghosts appear, making sense of some of the traits my siblings, my cousins and I have inherited. On my paternal side our grandparents came over to England from Russia and Lithuania. My father's father was one of a large, distinguished-looking family; he was balding and bearded, upright and cultured. They were well-known in London among the Jewish community. The history of our surname is intriguing, but not unusual. When the family arrived by boat at the British port they were asked their name. Mis-understanding the question (for they probably spoke only Yiddish), they replied GRIEV (a small town in Russia), and since then our family name has been GRIEW.

Grandpa Solomon married a small, doughty lady from Lithuania. She was a superb seamstress (as was one of her daughters), gave him ten children and became the proverbial matriarch. I never knew Solomon but see in my son -- balding and bearded and wonderfully musical -- a throw-back to that generation. When, with his rabbinical looks, he plays the fiddle, dark eyes dancing, utterly at one with his instrument, I can almost see my ancestors at home in their shtetls (villages) once again.

Recollections

My introduction to Poland came about at my school in 1939 when we had to learn the words and tunes of all the Allies' national anthems. The Polish words made the most impression on me:

Poland's soul has not departed
Whilst we live to own her
What by might was taken from us
Might can yet recover
March, march Dgbrowski unto liberation
With your arms to lead us we will save the nation.

Time flowed by and in 1946 I met a Pole, his story the history of many. He was captured by the Russians and sentenced to two years' hard labour in Siberia. This was called a 'honeymoon sentence' -- the shortest sentence they gave. In 1941 he was released with other Poles to form a Polish Army under General Anders in Russia, under British Command. In 1944 he fought in the Battle of Monte Cassino on Hill 5. He was critically wounded and lost his leg, among other wounds. In 1946 a Polish Resettlement Corps was founded for two years. Jan was released in 1948 and we married in Bristol.

Somewhere around 1950 my husband discovered that two of his dear friends were living outside Bristol, in Lulsgate, on an ex-RAF wartime camp. They were his school friends, Anna and Adolf Jankowski, who had lived in his home town of Sarny Poland, before the war. Adolf had been a prisoner in Siberia and Anna with her three little children had been forced to go to Germany to work in a factory. We made contact and received an invitation to come for the weekend, the start of many happy times

together. In the camp they had their own little chapel and I met my first Roman Catholic priest, Father Ryszard Gruza. After Mass we went to Anna's and Adolf's for lunch. Father became our friend as well as a priest and after lunch they would sing old Polish songs. I knew very little Polish, but felt happy to be with friends.

On some occasions I would walk in the fields with their children and collect sorrel leaves, and when we returned Anna would make soup from the leaves and add sour cream (*smietanka*) and hard-boiled eggs. This *pyszna* was excellent and it became my favourite soup. During conversation, my husband mentioned that they had traced his family in Sarny through the Red Cross. Could Anna trace her adopted mother in Russia? When she was found they applied for a visa, which was granted because she was over seventy years old, and no longer able to work. She had saved about 2,000 roubles in the Moscow Bank but was told by the bank cashier 'you can have it if you come back to Russia'.

She lived in Bristol until she was over ninety years, supported by Anna and Adolf and was buried in Holy Souls Cemetery, Brislington. She never learned English, and always longed for her home town. She also had been forced to go to Siberia, where she spent four years. When she was released, she returned home to Sarny and found her house reduced to rubble.

Through Anna and Adolf we have met other dear friends, Henryka and Henryk and their three children. The youngest, Edward, was my husband's godson. We meet on special family occasions and in the Polish church on Sundays. After Mass our conversation usually turns to Lulsgate, when we were all poor, but happy to be together as a family with enough food to eat.

Polish Catholic Church, Bristol

Thelma Ryczko was born in Newton Abbot, Devon in 1926 and married Jan Ryczko, a Polish political refugee, in Bristol in 1948. Thelma has recently attended courses on Deaf Awareness at Bristol University, Lip-reading and Speaking at the Deaf Centre and has attained a GCSE from Filton College for Reading and Listening. She attends a Polish Conversation course along with English through Drama and Dressmaking. Thelma attends these courses in order to improve her communication skills and satisfy her thirst for knowledge.

CARLOS LAPRIDA

From Santiago to Bristol

You are Chilean and came to England about ten years ago after living in various parts of Europe. How did you find living in Bristol?

I had always lived in big cities. Where I come from, Santiago, is an over-populated city. When I left in 1984, the whole population of the country was eleven million -- and about six million of those lived in Santiago, a city built for only three million people.

And I lived in Rome for a time, that's big, and in Greece, in Athens, an incredible city, one of the worst in the world, so over-populated and polluted, and I've been in Rotterdam with loads of people ... and suddenly here I was in Bristol, quite small by comparison, not crowded, and surrounded by green, open fields and quiet country lanes.

Do you remember the date when you came to England. Is it etched on your memory?

Yes, June 24th, 1989. It's the day when I celebrate my name, St Juan, back in Chile. Here it's a different kind of celebration, in Chile we celebrate the birthday and the Christian name. Absolutely everyone does. The 23rd is the night when people, even those who are not called Juan, do different tricks, like Halloween. People put three potatoes under the bed -- one has its skin, one is half-peeled, and one is peeled completely, and you keep them there until the next morning, on the 24th, you reach down without looking and pick one up -- and whichever one you have in your hand, will show you what your luck will be in the next year! If it's the one that's completely peeled, you probably are not going to be so lucky ... and so on. This is a common belief. It's been a country tradition for such a long time, that almost everyone does it. But probably after they have done it they wonder why!

So you were born in crowded Santiago. Did that make people more friendly, because of the closeness?

Yes, you have to get on with your friends and everyone. It's a way of making life easier. We already had a difficult life, we are an under-developed country, so you have to make the best of it. We are well known for it, we talk to absolutely everyone, make friends very easily.

Is the English character completely opposite? I remember you telling me about your first experience of the traditional Sunday lunch in Bristol ...

The so-called Sunday lunch! I think it's just a waste of time and space! My first Sunday lunch in England was an opportunity to meet my ex-girl friend's family for the first time. Well, everybody arrived, said, 'hello, nice to meet you,' lunch was ready so everybody took theirs and went to different rooms in the house! Some took their plates to the front room, some to the garden, some to the bedroom. I thought what is the point of having a Sunday lunch when everyone is sitting in a different room? In my country, when we get together for lunch -- we get together! There is a common belief that Chile is a disorganised country, but we are very organised over something like this! We have very large families, and when three families get together there will be about at least twenty kids -- enough to make more than one football team. All the children will eat first, and then we send them out to play, and it's time then for us, the adults. And it's more friendly. We talk, and every now and again there is a big fight, that's within us as well. We don't refrain from throwing a punch at anyone because it's just the way we are! And I think somehow it's better.

Somewhat different to the English! Is it that we are too cold, too distant, or too formal, or that we just don't have time to talk?

A bit 'too' of everything. If there is a problem between a family, for instance, people must speak to each other, and try to find a solution. Here it seems you go your way and I go my way, and that's it. We're not going to speak for the next twenty years of our lives, and that is always digging deep in your hearts ... while in my country, you have a row, you thump someone in the face, then you shake hands, go for a drink and everyone is happy. Not happy with the fight itself, but you express yourself that way. The fights last for a very short time -- of course, there are always exceptions, I know of some instances where disputes last a life time ...

Do you think that because you come from not just another country but another continent there is a huge difference in the way people think and feel here?

Absolutely. Even countries within Europe and within South America. I have had the good fortune to have travelled about quite a bit. You find that two neighbouring countries will be similar but at the same time very different because of their traditions and beliefs. This country is no exception.

Is your heart still in Chile?

Not just my heart, which will always be there, but my mind is always there, too. I am very proud to be Chilean. I can never forget my country -- it's as simple as that. I think this happens to many, many people who leave their country. They don't realise how much they love it until

they leave. In the beginning it was very, very difficult for me and I just learned to cope with it.

Were Bristol people curious about where you came from?

Yes, they are very curious. Most of the time people guess wrongly. The first association is with Spain because of my accent, and then it's Mexico, because a lot of people here don't know any further than that! What they know about South America is Brazil and they know that a high proportion of the population there is black -- and I'm not black, so the next possibility is Argentina, the only other South American country known here because of the Falklands War and the football.

Only in the last few years here people are beginning to know a little bit more about South America. Talking about Peru, for example, because people are now going for holidays -- visiting Machupichu and other places. Ecuador has become quite popular. It's not just English people. In Holland, a woman said, 'You come from South America'. Spot on, but now which country? And she added, 'from Mexico' -- the north of Central America!

Do you think you are taking on English characteristics now, because you've been here some years?

I feel like saying, definitely not. But people who know me would say yes! If you live somewhere long enough you obviously pick up mannerisms. I learned some English before I came. I used to speak with my 'h's all the time, but now I don't. I don't drink much tea, but I do now and again go with the old fish and chips.

I am always cooking Chilean food. But what I do miss a lot is my mum's and sister's cooking. The best in the world.

So your family are still in Chile. Do you feel isolated?

Yes, I'm the only one from my family who lives here. Isolation? It depends what you mean. Sometimes I feel people push me to one side, sometimes I do it myself because I want to keep my own beliefs and traditions. But I do believe as well that if I come to live in a foreign country I must try to live under their rules, regulations and traditions, and respect them for what they are -- as well as thanking them for letting me be part of their society. At the same time, I wouldn't like to be denied my own traditions.

You photograph wildlife -- you must miss your own landscape and climate?

I never knew how rich my country was in wildlife and never took much notice of the geography itself until I left. Because I was born there, I took it for granted. But since I have left my country, so many other places are nice, but I compare everywhere with my country, and that has made me think -- Chile is really beautiful and I should be proud of it.

Do you have an inner strength from having travelled so far and created your own life in a strange environment?

My inner strength I get mainly from people who want to deny foreign people -- who want to deny that I exist, as such, as a human being. They give me the strength and the courage to say no, I am not going to allow you -- because I am here and I exist.

Do you have to prove yourself all the time, and be better than the native English?

In the beginning, yes I did. I had very unpleasant experiences with British people. I have been pointed at many times, and have been subjected to all sorts of remarks. It was very difficult in the beginning.

Why do you think we are like that?

I don't know. It may be because most British people have the pre-conceived idea that anybody who comes to their country from abroad comes to make money, and take their jobs, their houses, their women, take something away. But that is not always the case. But if you go back in history you did it a long time before us -- you could say we are just kind of getting something back ... On the other hand, why should you pay for something that people did two hundred years ago?

England has this reputation as being a democracy and tolerant, but the reality for lots of people is different -- even, for some, huge amounts of racism. It's the norm for some people who are actually British and born here.

Yes, but where would we be without racism? It gave me the strength to keep going. Maybe if I never came across it, I would have to try and find my courage from something else. In the beginning I used to fight back and get aggressive -- even fight, physically. But I have learned that this is not the most important thing in life. If you want to believe you are better than me, fair enough, you can be 'better' than everybody! So what? Is it true?

Have you got strength from the Chilean community in Bristol?

Yes, the Chilean community is there, and will always help out if you are in trouble. They will always do something to help, sometimes enconomically if necessary. There are people who have helped me lots, and I am very grateful to them.

And what about cultural identity?

When Chileans came here as little children, say at five years old, they forgot everything. Now they are becoming teenagers and reaching adulthood, they are living in a culture that is not alien to them -- it's the only culture they know, and they go with it. Fortunately for them, their parents are there to remind them about their own country. It's not a question of making them study Chilean history, but putting in their minds that there is another part of them they don't know about.

I know a lot of teenagers who go on a Friday or Saturday night to a club and dance this very British or American dance music, but on a Wednesday they will go and dance salsa! I think this is very encouraging, they are not denying their culture.

It's important because these cultures contribute to this country. It's such a positive thing but it can so easily be turned into a negative because people are frightened of the unusual. People bring these gifts -- which we don't always realise are there -- like food, music, ideas, literature ...

Absolutely, yes. The main thing with these youngsters is that they are not being forced. They are being given

the choice and they are taking it.

That generation has such a unique thing, having two cultures.

Yes, but it can be destructive, too. If ever there comes a time and they have to decide, it will be very hard to take one side.

Will you go back to Chile?

At the moment, no. I went back some years ago, on holiday. But now I live very much on a day-to-day basis. I do what is best at the time. Maybe it's wrong, maybe it's right.

Do you think your philosophy comes from being a long way from home, and not rooted?

Yes, you meet new people who all believe in different ideas and religions, you do change your mind about things, you separate the good from the bad. You don't consciously change your point of view, but you realise your limitations.

The most important thing is you get to know new people and you understand how people think from different backgrounds. It's very important. I feel it is important to know not just about your own people, your own race -- but who is out there.

[Interview with **Geraldine Edwards**]

Carlos Laprida was born in Santiago, Chile in 1962, the youngest of three brothers. After living in different European countries, he came to Britain in 1989 where he studied at Filton College, Bristol, joined several photographic clubs, among them Bristol Photographic Society where he was awarded a number of prizes. He enjoys all kinds of sport, geography and wildlife.

SHAWN NAPHTALI SOBERS
Silent Witness

Mortley Grant sat in his chair. Every time he blinked it took just that little bit longer for his eyes to re-open, and each time they opened just that little bit narrower.

The etches in his ebony-tone skin fell deep with time. Seventy years previous this was virgin skin, cradled by his mother's love and untouched by breath. He was then born into this world. Age began its relentless pace. This skin has encased his soul on all its travels. Now it was time for his soul to travel alone.

Mortley was a tall heavy man. His sturdy armchair carried his weight well. Dusty green, frayed at every edge. Armchair knew Mortley well, maybe better than anyone. The wooden ends of each of its arms sported four worn spots in its varnish, from the constant drumming of Mortley's well worked finger tips. Particularly in these latter years, Mortley would sit in front of a switched-off television set and stare at the blank screen. To an observer he would appear to be waiting. Waiting for the phone to ring, the door to knock. Armchair felt it knew what Mortley waited for, even though Mortley himself never knew. Whenever Mortley sat in Armchair and thought, Armchair knew he was praying. What Mortley really waited for was God.

Mrs Grant once bought a brand-new three-piece suite. Mortley insisted that Armchair stayed. From that day onwards Armchair felt indebted to its owner, and paid Mortley back in the only way it knew how. Always be there for him. There was one day in particular that this relationship intensified considerably. This was the day the spirit of the room changed. The movement slowed. The talking stopped. Mortley Grant was now, officially, alone.

The living room stayed as it did in the time of Mrs Grant. Her glasses still rested on the mantle-piece. Flowery slippers discreetly placed by the side of one of the new chairs, next to the wool box. Adjacent to this was Armchair.

If Armchair was ever moved for any reason, which was unlikely, the carpet would expose four dents so worn in its surface the floorboards could be felt through the underlay. Mortley never felt the need to re-arrange anything. He left that kind of activity to Mrs Grant, and she also wasn't fond of drastic change. Maybe a new vase in spring, a change of curtains in the summer. Once every couple of years she would initiate a sabbatical indulgence, the last time being, of course, the new chairs. The flowered wallpaper was the next thing on the hit list, but that was before ...

Mortley hated the wallpaper when it was first put up ten years in memory. He frowned every time he looked at the entwining pastel flower stems which repeated every third row. Mrs Grant was always the more vocal presence of the two, and simply said, 'you'll get used to it.' She was right.

Mortley found himself thinking of Tyrone, his only grandchild, whenever he concentrated on the now faded wall covering. When the child was only three or four years old, he was fascinated by the flow of the shapes and colour. He would sit and try and draw the patterns using his gnarled Crayola crayons and imagination. That was one of the reasons the wallpaper had stayed up so long. Mortley would sit forward in Armchair watching, fascinated by the child's patience and attention to detail. Mortley then began to find himself trying to search for the same interest in the wallpaper that this child so obviously found in its

SARFRA RHAM

patterned arrangement. There was no denying the pattern was mildly interesting in a bland way, but Mortley could never recreate the aura in himself with which Tyrone seemed to approach the wallpaper each time, with new eyes. Mortley thanked the Lord for children's innocence and sense of wonder, a trait which adults rarely possess.

The alcove of the fire-side wall was covered almost completely in old photographs and postcards. Only a hint of wallpaper could be glimpsed through the gaps in the Blu-Tak'd pictures. This was the feature which caused the most excitement in the visitors to the house, even the regulars. The tiled 1950s fireplace and mantle were framed in a wonderful overlapping array of clashing colours and images. This was something which Mr and Mrs Grant were most proud of in their home, and by which their children were most embarrassed.

Constantly the three now-adult children would try to persuade their parents to redecorate, although none of them even lived at home any more. Once Beverly, the mother of Tyrone, took it upon herself to buy ten rolls of wallpaper and went as far as hiring the decorators to do the job. Needless to say, her parents turned them away without hesitation. The wallpaper stayed in the cellar for years and the nagging continued until Mrs Grant conceded and said she would agree to have the living room redecorated, but only when she was ready. She half said it just to keep the children quiet, even though she also reluctantly admitted to herself it was probably time for a change. Mrs Grant's submission came just two weeks before she passed on. The subject has never been raised since.

The Album Wall, as it was affectionately called, could spark hours of colourful conversations and stories about Barbados and the 'old times'. This was one of the reasons the house was such a magnet for friends who were 'just passing by'. Hours later the elders would still be reminiscing and recounting the funny tales of Home.

'What did ever 'appen to ole Swing Foot Jones?'

'He mus' dead now fa true.'

'No he ain' dead yet! Aunt Lou se she pass he by Bibby's Lane when she did home de las' time.'

'Fi true? Well praise de Lord. Swing Foot mus' be in he nineties now innit? I did t'ink he did dead ever since. Praise de Lord.'

'Nineties? I hear he already pass t'rough he hundredth birt'day, ya know.'

'Fi true?'

'Praise de Lord!'

The conversations would meander and journey into the small hours of the night. When the friends had left and Mr and Mrs Grant laid down to sleep, nothing could stop dreams from entertaining the night. It was on such a night which Mrs Grant floated to her Father's Home.

Mortley relaxed in Armchair and drummed his fingers against the varnished grain. He cast his eyes over the Album Wall and closed them to meditate under the solitude and stillness of his eyelids. The thud of four fingers was the only sound.

Among the images on the wall were postcards from Barbados, Jamaica, America, Cornwall, Leicester, The Isle of Wight, Bath, Bristol, London, France, Morocco and Amsterdam. These were from their children, friends, relatives, old work-friends, and some bought by Mrs Grant herself because she simply liked the picture on them. The photographs told the story of generations. Photographs taken on the day of their wedding 48 years ago were pinned side-by-side with Tyrone's school photographs and his mother's, aunt's and uncle's baby pictures. There was no obvious order to the wall, not as may be found in a photo album book. Images from day trips were scattered on all corners, likewise with 'event' photos such as weddings and christenings. Mortley and Mrs Grant knew exactly where each photograph was without really realising the skill involved. The wallpaper on either side of the alcove carried the repetitive pattern of flowers. The Album Wall, however, carried the fragmented chaos of sweet memories.

The last memory Mortley saw before he closed his eyes was that of his mother.

The sepia-toned photograph showed a woman heavy in stature and gentle in eyes. She stood uncomfortably straight and stiff-backed clutching a handbag. Her Sunday-hat tilted slightly as she shifted to find a natural pose.

'Mama. Keep still nuh! I wan' fi tek one more so I can sen' it back fi ya.'

'Wha I wan' pic'cha of mi self fa? You know se mi own a mirror already!'

Mama relentlessly paced over to Mortley and adjusted the collar of his shirt and blazer.

'Fru time you reach Englan' you haf' fi save ya money, ya hear? If anyt'ing you sen' back, mek it a likkle money fi ya bruddah an sista, ya hear?'

Mortley rescued his clothes from his mother's clutches and put his arm around her.

'Listen mama. I gon' miss ya, ya know dat. Tek care of ya self.'

Mama discreetly escaped her son's embrace. She was never a person to outwardly show her emotions, particularly if she was sad. Mortley knew her ways well and wasn't offended. He kept a firm hold of her earth-hardened hands.

'Listen.'

Mama spoke in a matter-of-fact manner.

'Don't even bod' da worrying 'bout me. It's you dat ya haf' fi look afta', ya hear? The Lord protec' me in all I do, an' I pray Him will look afta' you in Englan'. Have faith an' de Lord will be wid you. You know I always tell ya dat.'

Mama snatched back her hand and rummaged around in her handbag.

'Mama, mi know dat but ...'

Mama wouldn't let him speak.

'Look 'ere! I wan' you fi tek dis. Ya know how I does treasure it, so when you done mek ya money an' come back in five years, I wan' ya fi give dis back in de same condition as mi give it to ya, ya hear?'

Mama handed Mortley a book which was as much a part of the family as anyone.

'I c'yan tek ya Bible frum ya Mama. When I reach Englan' I'll buy one, mi promise.'

'Chuh! Just tek what mi give ya an' hush ya mout'. I put ya in Jesus trust frum now. Ya bes' pray an' show your appreciation to de Father.'

Mortley was told.

'T'ank ya mama. Mi love ya.'

'Love de Lord!'

Mortley kissed his mother on the cheek and slowly parted.

'I haf' fi go now. De ship soon lef'.'

'Well tek dis now before ya lef it. God be wid ya my son. I pray fi ya.'

Mortley took the Bible, picked up his small suitcase and left for the New World.

Mortley sat in Armchair. The trusty friend carried his weight well. The wooden varnished ends felt the texture of its master's worn, still left hand. The movement ceased. The thudding stopped. The spirit of the room changed. Armchair was now, officially, alone.

Armchair knew quietly it wasn't strictly alone. There was still one dedicated companion which Armchair had always known. A heavy book which always lived on its right arm. Mortley's hand was tightly clutched around the rough leather-bound cover. His nails were dug deep into the well thumbed pages of text. He waited no longer. Mortley had finally floated to his Father's Home.

Shawn Naphtali Sobers is a local writer and film maker. Since graduating from University of Wales College, Newport he has worked extensively with Black Pyramid Films and works as a Technical Workshop Leader at HTV Studios. Shawn drew inspiration for this writing from his own roots in Barbados. It is dedicated to his parents, his brother and sister and Cee.

"*I miss my work. I miss the stars at night and being out in the air. I miss being barefoot – I hate having to wear shoes on my feet.*"

Bristol Somali schoolboy who used to look after camels

CHRISTINA MALKOWSKA ZABA

Crossing the Caspian Sea to Persia

When I was a little girl in Manchester in the 1960s, my mother often used to tell me about her exile from Poland to the USSR as a child in the war, and her travels on through Persia to India and then England. She used to get cross when we asked for things we didn't have.

'Don't you become like these English people who think that the only thing that matters is the next house or the next car,' she would say. 'My God, if they'd been invaded they'd think differently. Imagine it. The soldiers come for you at three in the morning. You're living in a house full of family portraits, silver, fine furniture, everything. And they tell you you're going to Siberia and you have exactly half an hour to pack. What do you take?' We knew the list: furs and boots for warmth, photo album for memories, jewellery to barter, food in bags, fear and courage and hopes and prayers.

'And when you leave the house and close the door behind you,' she'd continue, 'you know that you'll never see it again. Not ever. And you know what? At that moment you're just grateful that you're all alive, and that you have your children by the hand, and something to eat. Nothing else is important. Not really. I remember,' she went on, 'how ill I was as a child when there was the amnesty and the Russians let us Poles go. We had a month to get out of Kazakhstan and across the Caspian Sea to Tehran in Persia. Just a month, and all those people. And there weren't many ships. I was so ill, I begged them to leave me behind; but they made me get up and run on to the ship. It was such a hot day, with the most beautiful blue sky, and there was a wide sandy beach running down to the water, and the people crowding up on to the gang-plank. And soldiers at the top of the gang-

plank. They were so handsome in their uniforms,' she mused, 'and they were ordering the people to hurry, and to leave everything behind and just get on.

'There was no room for luggage, just for people. So everyone was dropping all their bags and bundles there on the sand and crowding up to get on the ship and get away to the free world. And I remember the sand was hot, and it was very prickly and hurting my feet. And when I looked down I saw why.

'I was walking on a path of gold and silver. There were precious jewels, fantastic treasures, family heirlooms. You can't imagine the diamonds and necklaces and bracelets and cups and caskets that were lying there in the sand getting trampled. I still remember how I looked around and it seemed to me that the whole huge beach was one big carpet of gold and silver, glittering in the sun, leading to that ship. And that was what was cutting my feet. You see,' she explained, 'people had saved their most precious valuables right through Siberia, and now they had to leave it all behind. So they just dropped it, there and then. And the people behind had to walk over it. And do you know what? No one cared. No one.

'You should always remember,' she ended, 'however nice money is, don't make the mistake of thinking that it matters. What matter is your life.'

[As told by **Janina Malkowska**]

Christina Malkowska Zaba is 39 years old, a lecturer at Bristol University for Continuing Education, an editor and journalist. She has a husband and two children, grew up in Manchester but is now settled in Bristol. Her mother, Janina Malkowska, was born in Poland in 1927, was a primary school teacher with three children.

Looking Back

Mrs Suporan: I first moved to Manchester from India. My father, my older and younger brother were also there. So we lived there for ten years. When we came, my mum and my sister-in-law would sit in the whole time. I would say, 'why don't you go out?' They would say, 'we don't know the speak.' I'd say, 'if you don't know how to speak, we can still look.'

So we went to town, because we needed eggs to prepare the food. Dad had been delayed at work and couldn't come. I wanted to cook eggs and potato curry. I usually took a young boy with me and he would help with the English. This time, I went alone and tried to explain to the shopkeeper what I wanted. I made a circular shape with my hands and she brought out potatoes, then she brought out onions. She showed me this and that. So then, finally, I started clucking like a chicken and she got the message and brought the eggs out. So I managed to buy one dozen eggs and she had already shown me the onions and potatoes, which I also bought. When I got home my mother, dad and brother had a good laugh and said, 'look how clever our girl is. We've been here a year and never left the house, she hasn't even been here for two months and has already gone out and done the shopping.'

I also wanted to take my mother and sister-in-law to the town centre. They said, 'how are we going to do that?' So I wrote down our home address on a piece of paper, so that if we got lost we could at least get a taxi home. So we got on the bus, and I said to the driver, 'we want to go to town', and he took the money and we got on.

Kishan Kaur: I came to England in 1957, when I was 15 years old. We came by boat from India as in those days aeroplanes weren't that common. I was going to England to get married, so we had brought lots of luggage with us. I got married a year later in Doncaster.

It wasn't possible in those days to get much here that was Asian. In those days there were no gudurahs [Sikh temples] so we got married at home. My mum had the five of us, we've all seen a lot of hardship, but not as much as our parents went through to come to England. They sold their houses and possessions and with teenage children came to settle in another country. The English -- some were good, but there were also not-so-nice people among them. There were many who were prejudiced, many good, but mainly prejudiced. When you stood next to someone, they would say they smelt curry and garlic. At the time, you couldn't even get garlic in England!

When I got married it was very unusual to have an Asian wedding in England, and we got a lot of attention from the media, lots of photographs for the newspapers.

Anon: When I first arrived in 1962, there were not many Asian families in Manchester -- there were only four houses. One my mother lived in, one me and one each for my two brothers. In Bristol we moved first to Lawrence Hill. It was a popular place at the time, it was a very good area, and my older brother got a house there.

It was difficult to find Asian food, but we managed because a truck used to come from London -- it was owned by Asian people -- and from it you could buy chicken, lamb, rice, chappati flour, to last you a month. There were Asian shops in Manchester, but in Bristol none

at that time. In Manchester, it was difficult, my heart just wouldn't take. It was very cold in Manchester, but I never really felt the cold; others did, but I didn't. But now I am old, I feel the cold, and gradually I've picked up English.

[Contributed by members of the **Sikh Resource Centre** speaking to **Jamila Yousaf**]

Mrs SUPORAN, KISHAN KAUR and Anon

ਪਿਛਾਂਹ ਝਾਤ

ਮਿਸਿਜ਼ ਸੁਪੋਰਨ: ਇੰਡੀਆ ਤੋਂ ਸਭਤੋਂ ਪਹਿਲਾਂ ਮੈਂ ਮਾਨਚੈਸਟਰ ਆਈ। ਮੇਰੇ ਪਿਤਾ ਜੀ, ਵੱਡੇ ਅਤੇ ਛੋਟੇ ਭਰਾ ਵੀ ਉੱਥੇ ਹੀ ਸਨ। ਇਸ ਲਈ ਅਸੀ ਉੱਥੇ ਦਸ ਸਾਲ ਰਹੇ। ਜਦ ਅਸੀ ਆਏ ਤਾਂ ਮੇਰੀ ਮਾਂ ਅਤੇ ਭਰਜਾਈ ਸਾਰਾ ਦਿਨ ਘਰੇ ਬੈਠੀਆਂ ਰਹਿੰਦੀਆਂ ਸਨ। ਮੈਂ ਕਹਿੰਦੀ ਰਹਿੰਦੀ – "ਤੁਸੀ ਬਾਹਰ ਕਿਉਂ ਨਹੀ ਜਾਂਦੀਆਂ?" ਪਰ ਉਹਨਾਂ ਦਾ ਜਵਾਬ ਹੁੰਦਾ – "ਸਾਨੂੰ ਗੱਲ ਕਰਨੀ ਨਹੀ ਆਉਂਦੀ।" ਮੈਂ ਕਹਿੰਦੀ – "ਤੁਸੀ ਬੋਲ ਨਹੀ ਸਕਦੀਆਂ; ਪਰ ਅਸੀ ਦੇਖ ਤਾਂ ਸਕਦੀਆਂ ਹਾਂ।"

ਇਸ ਲਈ ਅਸੀ ਸ਼ਹਿਰ ਵਿਚ ਨੂੰ ਨਿਕਲ ਪਈਆਂ, ਕਿਉਂਕਿ ਖਾਣਾ ਬਨਾਉਣ ਕਰਨ ਲਈ ਆਂਡੇ ਚਾਹੀਦੇ ਸਨ। ਪਿਤਾ ਜੀ ਨੂੰ ਕੰਮ ਤੇ ਦੇਰ ਹੋ ਗਈ ਸੀ, ਅਤੇ ਉਹ ਆ ਨਹੀ ਸਕੇ ਸਨ। ਮੈਂ ਆਲੂਆਂ ਅਤੇ ਆਂਡਿਆਂ ਦੀ ਭੁਰਜੀ ਬਨਾਉਣਾ ਚਾਹੁੰਦੀ ਸਾਂ। ਆਮ ਤੌਰ ਤੇ ਮੈਂ ਕਿਸੇ ਛੋਟੇ ਜਿਹੇ ਮੁੰਡੇ ਨੂੰ ਨਾਲ ਲੈ ਜਾਇਆ ਕਰਦੀ ਸਾਂ, ਅਤੇ ਉਹ ਅੰਗਰੇਜ਼ੀ ਬੋਲ ਕੇ ਮੇਰੀ ਮਦਦ ਕਰ ਦਿੰਦਾ ਸੀ। ਪਰ ਇਸ ਵਾਰੀ ਮੈਂ ਇਕੱਲੀ ਗਈ ਅਤੇ ਦੁਕਾਨਦਾਰ ਨੂੰ ਸਮਝਾਉਣ ਦੀ ਕੋਸ਼ਿਸ਼ ਕੀਤੀ ਕਿ ਮੈਨੂੰ ਕੀ ਚਾਹੀਦਾ ਹੈ। ਮੈਂ ਹੱਥਾਂ ਨਾਲ ਗੋਲ ਜਿਹੀ ਚੀਜ਼ ਦਾ ਇਸ਼ਾਰਾ ਕੀਤਾ ਅਤੇ ਉਹ ਆਲੂ ਲੈ ਆਈ, ਫਿਰ ਉਹ ਗੰਢੇ ਲਿਆਈ। ਉਹਨੇ ਮੈਨੂੰ ਕਈ ਚੀਜ਼ਾਂ ਦਿਖਾਈਆਂ। ਤਦ ਅਖੀਰ ਵਿਚ ਜਦ ਮੈਂ ਕੁਕੜੀ ਵਾਂਗ ਕੁੜ ਕੁੜ ਕਰਨ ਲੱਗੀ, ਤਾਂ ਉਹਨੂੰ ਗੱਲ ਸਮਝ ਆ ਗਈ ਅਤੇ ਉਹ ਆਂਡੇ ਲੈ ਆਈ। ਇੰਝ ਮੈਂ ਇਕ ਦਰਜਨ ਆਂਡੇ ਖਰੀਦ ਲਏ। ਉਹਨੇ ਮੇਰੇ ਲਈ ਆਲੂ ਅਤੇ ਗੰਢੇ ਪਹਿਲਾਂ ਹੀ ਲਿਆਂਦੇ ਹੋਏ ਸਨ, ਮੈਂ ਉਹ ਵੀ ਖਰੀਦ ਲਏ। ਜਦ ਮੈਂ ਘਰ ਪਹੁੰਚੀ ਤਾਂ ਮੇਰੀ ਮਾਂ, ਪਿਤਾ ਅਤੇ ਭਰਾ ਖੂਬ ਹੱਸੇ ਅਤੇ ਬੋਲੇ – "ਦੇਖੋ ਸਾਡੀ ਕੁੜੀ ਕਿੰਨੀ ਸਿਆਣੀ ਹੈ। ਅਸੀ ਸਾਲ ਭਰ ਤੋਂ ਇੱਥੇ ਰਹਿ ਰਹੇ ਹਾਂ, ਅਤੇ ਕਦੇ ਘਰੋਂ ਬਾਹਰ ਨਹੀ ਨਿਕਲੇ; ਇਹਨੂੰ ਆਇਆਂ ਹਾਲੇ ਦੋ ਮਹੀਨੇ ਵੀ ਨਹੀ ਹੋਏ, ਪਰ ਇਹਨੇ ਜਾ ਕੇ ਚੀਜ਼ਾਂ ਵੀ ਖਰੀਦ ਲਈਆਂ।"

ਮੈਂ ਆਪਣੀ ਮਾਂ ਅਤੇ ਭਰਜਾਈ ਨੂੰ ਵੀ ਟਾਊਨ ਸੈਂਟਰ ਵਿਚ ਲਿਜਾਣਾ ਚਾਹੁੰਦੀ ਸਾਂ। ਉਹ ਕਹਿਣ ਲੱਗੀਆਂ – "ਅਸੀ ਇਹ ਕੰਮ ਕਿੱਦਾਂ ਕਰਾਂਗੀਆਂ?" ਇਸ ਲਈ ਮੈਂ ਕਾਗਜ਼ ਤੇ ਘਰ ਦਾ ਪਤਾ ਲਿਖ ਕੇ ਰੱਖ ਲਿਆ, ਤਾਂ ਕਿ ਜੇ ਅਸੀ ਗੁਆਚ ਗਈਆਂ ਤਾਂ ਘੱਟੋ ਘੱਟ ਟੈਕਸੀ ਫੜ ਕੇ ਘਰ ਤਾਂ ਪਹੁੰਚ ਜਾਵਾਂਗੀਆਂ। ਫਿਰ ਅਸੀ ਬਸ ਵਿਚ ਵੜ ਕੇ ਡਰਾਈਵਰ ਨੂੰ ਕਿਹਾ, "ਵੀ ਵਾਂਟ ਟੂ ਗੋ ਟੂ ਟਾਊਨ।" ਉਹਨੇ ਪੈਸੇ ਫੜ ਲਏ, ਅਤੇ ਅਸੀ ਬਸ ਫੜ ਲਈ।

ਕਿਸ਼ਨ ਕੌਰ: ਮੈਂ 1957 ਵਿਚ ਇੰਗਲੈਂਡ ਆਈ, ਜਦ ਮੈਂ 15 ਸਾਲਾਂ ਦੀ ਸਾਂ। ਇੰਡੀਆ ਤੋਂ ਅਸੀ ਸਮੁੰਦਰੀ ਜਹਾਜ਼ ਵਿਚ ਆਏ, ਕਿਉਂਕਿ ਉਹਨਾਂ ਦਿਨਾਂ ਵਿਚ ਹਵਾਈ ਜਹਾਜ਼ ਇੰਨੇ ਜ਼ਿਆਦਾ ਨਹੀ ਸਨ ਹੁੰਦੇ। ਮੈਂ ਇੰਗਲੈਂਡ ਵਿਆਹ ਕਰਵਾਉਣ ਲਈ ਆ ਰਹੀ ਸਾਂ, ਇਸ ਲਈ ਸਾਡੇ ਕੋਲ ਕਾਫੀ ਸਾਮਾਨ ਸੀ। ਬਾਅਦ ਵਿਚ ਮੇਰਾ ਵਿਆਹ ਡੌਨਕਾਸਟਰ ਵਿਚ ਹੋਇਆ।

ਉਹਨੀ ਦਿਨੀ ਏਸ਼ੀਅਨ ਚੀਜ਼ਾਂ ਇੱਥੇ ਐਨੀਆਂ ਨਹੀ ਸਨ ਮਿਲਦੀਆਂ। ਗੁਰਦੁਆਰੇ ਵੀ ਨਹੀ ਸਨ, ਇਸ ਲਈ ਸਾਡਾ ਵਿਆਹ ਘਰ ਵਿਚ ਹੀ ਹੋਇਆ। ਮੇਰੀ ਮਾਂ ਦੇ ਪੰਜ ਬੱਚੇ ਸਨ, ਅਤੇ ਅਸੀ ਸਭਨਾਂ ਨੇ ਬੜੇ ਔਖੇ ਦਿਨ ਦੇਖੇ ਹਨ, ਪਰ ਅਸੀ ਐਨੀਆਂ ਔਕੜਾਂ ਨਹੀ ਝੱਲੀਆਂ ਜਿੰਨੀਆਂ ਸਾਡੇ ਮਾਪਿਆਂ ਨੇ ਇੰਗਲੈਂਡ ਆਉਣ ਲਈ ਝੱਲੀਆਂ ਹਨ। ਉਹ ਘਰ ਬਾਰ ਵੇਚ ਕੇ ਚੜ੍ਹਦੀ ਉਮਰ ਦੇ ਬੱਚਿਆਂ ਨੂੰ ਲੈ ਕੇ ਪਰਦੇਸ ਵਿਚ ਰਹਿਣ ਆ ਗਏ। ਗੋਰੇ ਲੋਕਾਂ ਵਿਚ ਕੁਝ ਚੰਗੇ ਵੀ ਸਨ, ਅਤੇ ਕੁਝ ਘੱਟ ਚੰਗੇ ਵੀ। ਬਹੁਤਿਆਂ ਦੇ ਵਿਚਾਰ ਸਾਡੇ ਬਾਰੇ ਕਾਫੀ ਮਾੜੇ ਸਨ। ਕਈ ਗੋਰੇ ਚੰਗੇ ਤਾਂ ਸਨ, ਪਰ ਸਾਡੇ ਬਾਰੇ ਗਲਤ ਵਿਚਾਰ ਉਹਨਾਂ ਦੇ ਦਿਮਾਗ ਵਿਚ ਵੀ ਸਨ। ਜਦ ਤੁਸੀ ਕਿਸੇ ਦੇ ਕੋਲ ਖੜ੍ਹਦੇ ਤਾਂ ਉਹ ਕਹਿੰਦੇ ਕਿ ਕੜੀ ਅਤੇ ਲਸਣ ਦੀ ਮੁਸ਼ਕ ਆ ਰਹੀ ਹੈ। ਹਾਲਾਂਕਿ ਉਸ ਵੇਲੇ ਇੰਗਲੈਂਡ ਵਿਚ ਲਸਣ ਕਿਧਰੇ ਵੀ ਨਹੀ ਸੀ ਮਿਲਦਾ।

ਜਦ ਮੇਰਾ ਵਿਆਹ ਹੋਇਆ ਤਾਂ ਇੰਗਲੈਂਡ ਵਿਚ ਏਸ਼ੀਅਨ ਵਿਆਹ ਬੜੀ ਅਨੋਹਣੀ ਜਿਹੀ ਗੱਲ ਸੀ, ਅਤੇ ਮੀਡੀਆ ਦਾ ਧਿਆਨ ਸਾਡੇ ਵਲ ਕਾਫੀ ਗਿਆ, ਅਤੇ ਅਖਬਾਰਾਂ ਵਿਚ ਬੜੇ ਫੋਟੇ ਛਪੇ।

ਬੇਨਾਮ: ਜਦ ਅਸੀ 1962 ਵਿਚ ਇੰਗਲੈਂਡ ਆਏ ਤਾਂ ਮਾਨਚੈਸਟਰ ਵਿਚ ਬਹੁਤੇ ਏਸ਼ੀਅਨ ਪਰਿਵਾਰ ਨਹੀ ਸਨ – ਸਿਰਫ ਚਾਰ ਘਰ ਸਨ। ਇਕ ਵਿਚ ਮੇਰੀ ਮਾਂ ਰਹਿੰਦੀ ਸੀ, ਇਕ ਵਿਚ ਮੈਂ ਅਤੇ ਇਕ ਇਕ ਵਿਚ ਮੇਰੇ

ਭਰਾ। ਬ੍ਰਿਸਟਲ ਅਸੀਂ ਸਭ ਤੋਂ ਪਹਿਲਾਂ ਲਾਅਰੈਸ ਹਿੱਲ ਵਿਚ ਰਹੇ। ਉਹਨੀਂ ਦਿਨੀਂ ਇਹ ਥਾਂ ਕਾਫੀ ਪਸੰਦ ਕੀਤੀ ਜਾਂਦੀ ਸੀ. ਵਧੀਆ ਥਾਂ ਸੀ ਅਤੇ ਮੇਰੇ ਭਰਾਵਾਂ ਨੇ ਉੱਥੇ ਘਰ ਲੈ ਲਿਆ।

ਏਸ਼ੀਅਨ ਖਾਣਾ ਲੱਭਣਾ ਔਖਾ ਸੀ. ਪਰ ਅਸੀਂ ਕੰਮ ਚਲਾ ਲੈਂਦੇ ਸਾਂ. ਕਿਉਂਕਿ ਲੰਡਨੋਂ ਇਕ ਟਰੱਕ ਆਉਂਦਾ ਹੁੰਦਾ ਸੀ ਜਿਹਤੋਂ ਅਸੀਂ ਘੱਟੋ ਘੱਟ ਇਕ ਮਹੀਨੇ ਜੋਗਾ ਚਿਕਨ, ਲੈਮ ਅਤੇ ਚਪਾਤੀਆਂ ਦਾ ਆਟਾ ਖਰੀਦ ਲੈਂਦੇ ਸਾਂ। ਮਾਨਚੈਸਟਰ ਵਿਚ ਏਸ਼ੀਅਨ ਦੁਕਾਨਾਂ ਹੈ ਸਨ. ਪਰ ਬ੍ਰਿਸਟਲ ਵਿਚ ਉਸ ਵੇਲੇ ਕੋਈ ਨਹੀਂ ਸੀ। ਮਾਨਚੈਸਟਰ ਵਿਚ ਜ਼ਿੰਦਗੀ ਮੁਸ਼ਕਿਲ ਸੀ. ਮੇਰਾ ਦਿਲ ਨਹੀਂ ਸੀ ਲਗਦਾ। ਮਾਨਚੈਸਟਰ ਵਿਚ ਬੜੀ ਠੰਢ ਸੀ. ਪਰ ਮੈਨੂੰ ਕੋਈ ਖਾਸ ਠੰਢ ਮਹਿਸੂਸ ਨਹੀਂ ਸੀ ਹੁੰਦੀ, ਬਾਕੀਆਂ ਨੂੰ ਮਹਿਸੂਸ ਹੁੰਦੀ ਸੀ, ਪਰ ਮੈਨੂੰ ਨਹੀਂ। ਪਰ ਹੁਣ ਮੇਰੀ ਉਮਰ ਵਧ ਗਈ ਹੈ, ਅਤੇ ਠੰਢ ਵੀ ਲਗਣ ਲਗ ਪਈ ਹੈ। ਹੌਲੀ ਹੌਲੀ ਮੈਂ ਅੰਗਰੇਜ਼ੀ ਸਿੱਖ ਲਈ ਹੈ।

(ਸਿੱਖ ਰਿਜ਼ੋਰਸ ਸੈਂਟਰ ਦੇ ਮੈਂਬਰਾਂ ਨੇ ਜਮੀਲਾ ਯੂਸਫ਼ ਨੂੰ ਇਹ ਗੱਲਾਂ ਦੱਸੀਆਂ)

MARGARET GRIEW

Ring in the Old

1990. There is an accepted symbolism attached to the ending of a decade, a time to take stock, the opportunity for a personal rite of passage. In my case it seemed to signify a change of status within my peer group: many were recently retired, my closest friend had been widowed, some were reporting 'we are a grandmother' and I felt the need to seek the reassurance of roots. So this year we deserted our Bristol friends, with whom we have celebrated over the past fifteen years, and accepted an invitation to a New Year's party in London.

We had known most of our fellow guests for over thirty-five years and we have all kept in close touch since before any of us were married. In the early 1950s we were pretentiously intellectual, liked to think of ourselves as vaguely bohemian and had come together because we abhorred the conventional 'marriage market' clubs of north-west London Jewish society. Then our politics had been fiercely radical (some would say red); we are representative of fairly successful middle-aged, middle-class professional and business people and today the talk is mainly reactionary, although I hasten to add that some of us remain loyally socialist.

We were welcomed most warmly at the party. Conversation was easy, the atmosphere vibrant and noisy as it always is when this crowd of excitable personalities meet. I felt I had come home. Twenty-two of us sat round a table to eat long Vienna sausages and potato salad, followed by a Stilton and grapes, fruit salad and ice-cream, washed down with a superb '84 claret (our host had put down a case especially for this night). At midnight we drank champagne and danced. At one a.m.

there we were, sitting round the table again, eating and drinking once more. This time it was coffee and kuchen -- the word 'cake' would be too mundane to describe the fabulous array of confectionery which only the Austrian-born could produce.

Naturally talk became nostalgic. My supper neighbour and I were analysing the very special atmosphere of the room. As one we came to the explanation: a third of the people present had come to this country immediately before the second world war as refugees from the Nazis. One still bears a numbered tattoo from a concentration camp, his wife was, for a time, a hidden 'Anne Frank' child. One followed her father round Europe before settling here and remembers the park in Vienna where Jews were verboten. Another escaped with her mother and sister -- her father died in an unknown camp. Yet another came on kindertransport with hundreds of orphaned children. No wonder these people, and the rest of us who are their friends and spouses, have a need for the continuity and security of a group like ours. How good that we can come together as a surrogate extended family, warts and all (for feuds and backbiting occur as in the best of families).

There are two special dimensions which add to the ethos of this group. Firstly, there is an irrepressible sense of humour, joke telling of a high degree which elicits frequent and uncontrollable laughter. Secondly, I noticed that the amount of hugging and kissing taking place is far in excess of that seen elsewhere and that the women probably kissed and were kissed at least forty times each during the evening! We hope to go to a similar party on New Year's Eve 2000.

"I came to London first before Bristol from Zimbabwe and woke up on the first morning and watched everyone running from a fire. I ran out of where I was staying to run with them, but got confused when I asked them where the fire was. Nobody knew. The next day the same thing happened. And the next. They weren't running from a fire – they were rushing to work."

Bristol college lecturer

My name is Karen Chang and I was born in Kingston Town, Jamaica. My father's family came from China, but they fled to Jamaica when he was young because of a political revolution. My mother was born in England, but her origins were in Jamaica, where she spent a large part of her childhood.

I come from a large family of thirteen half-sisters and four half-brothers from my dad's side, but I grew up with only four sisters, just two of whom were in the household, with one brother. The others live in America or other parts of Jamaica.

My parents divorced when I was nine. My mum had been in a difficult situation. She was being abused by my father, but I was her daughter who needed to be looked after and all her money was in my dad's care. I wrote to my grandmother asking her to come over, and when she came to visit, plans were made so that if things did not improve, mum could flee to England with me.

We moved our belongings to a friend's house closer to the airport and mum told me not to let anyone know what was going to happen. One day she came to collect me from school and we went to the friend's house to pick up our things. When we got to the airport, dad was waiting with my two half-sisters and brother -- mum had said goodbye to them at the last moment, and they had told him. He asked her to stay, but she refused and he turned to me, holding my hand, and asked who I wanted to stay with. Because my ties were stronger with my mum, I went with her.

We settled with my grandmother in Easton, Bristol, leaving my brother and sisters in Jamaica. The loss of security within my family made me more aware of the world around me. I had been in a big family, where I was the youngest, and any other connections were family or friends of the family, and I had been educated privately at a Catholic school. So I had been very protected.

I continued a Catholic education in England, where I became fairly withdrawn because the people and their atttitudes were so different. I made few close friends, only three of whom I still keep in contact with. To me the environment seemed hostile and racist, and the girls and boys were very much separate, whereas in Jamaica everyone hung around together.

My mum met a man at her work-place, and they have been partners for the last nine years. He is white, of Spanish descent, brought up in Dorset, and has over the years become a close friend of mine as a step-father, although mum and he do not want to marry. They share a good understanding, because they have both been through rough marriages.

When mum had built up the finances, we moved to the outskirts of Bristol where I found very few people of colour. I was one of only five in my area and the people I met in school found me fascinating and asked about my accent, which was no longer Jamaican, and my culture and origins. My social life increased with the people I met there because I was no longer subject to the strict rules my grandmother enforced, like friends not being allowed around.

Looking back to this period in my life, I had mainly white friends, and I can see how I conformed to their ways so I could feel more comfortable. One harsh memory is of people holding a position of prestige in my peer group. An element of behaviour shown by someone popular was

St Pauls Carnival

often copied by the others, which in Jamaica was called 'follow fashion'. I broke these rules -- to me everyone was equal, and I could not participate in the bad talking of another group member just because she was considered lower down the hierarchy. As a result, my relations with the 'leader' of the group were very confused, and I felt outcast although everyone else was friendly.

In my teenage years, I focussed on study but in my eighteenth year my interests broadened, and I came into contact with many cultures, and had more freedom for new experiences and new places.

I have met with the Irish on the coast of Ireland, who seem to lead a simple, happy life in a very close-knit community. I have met a Chilean minority in Bristol who I feel are growing as part of my family because their values are so similar to mine, although their behaviour may be very different. Most are very loud when happy, loud when upset, loud when just talking and loud when arguing a point, but the thing I like most about them is that what you see is what you get. The older generation seem to have a lot of knowledge and a great many wise words, whereas my generation in that community, although they know principles, still try to get away with as much as possible.

I've met a few travellers who have seen a lot, some have done the things I want to do in my life -- like talk to American Indians, travel around the world, and give their efforts to helping under-developed countries. I've met those who pass on their knowledge of the wonders around the world and the mysteries of cultures encountered.

Many whom I've met seem very materialistic, concentrating more on what they can get from the world, or from manipulating other people. I have met other 'ethnics' of black and Asian backgrounds who have been brought up over here and question everything, but seem to have misplaced their roots. Then there are those with a similar mission to mine, a quest for a knowledge of the world and a better understanding of human nature. To me, what makes life so great is nature: humans play a part in its greatness and all the cultures and all the origins make it so special, but many do not appreciate this wonderful diversity.

I have experienced racism and prejudice from people of different cultures, as well as those who come from my own. Some don't see me as Chinese and others don't see me as Jamaican because I am not entirely one or the other, so I am not treated as their equal. I believe you make yourself who you want to be, and you should be proud of who you are, overcoming the wrongs of the past and cherishing the achievements. I feel privileged to be of mixed race, as it is the source of my open-mindedness, but I recognise that it is sometimes my downfall, when I merely sympathise with others who need my help, instead of sharing my knowledge with them to help make them stronger.

In my school days I studied the history of the Sioux nations. I admire so much their understanding of the need for balance and respect for people and nature. It is such a simple and joyful concept to me that it is forever part of my life. An example of what I mean is my decision to study, so I can concentrate on making my own contribution, in encouraging a more earth-friendly way of living. As well as travelling the world in my time out, I mean to come into contact with the cultures I admire. In this way, I feel I will get a good balance, nurturing mind and soul and getting as much out of life as I can.

I used to think that my strength in who I am and what I represent has diminished over the years of being brought up in a different culture -- the white culture -- but now I know that things develop as they will and if you know what is there, you can focus on bringing it into the foreground.

I believe that appreciating the gifts we have, and spreading them to others in an exchange of learning, is our way forward. I have recently met a member of a society called the Indigenous Youth. They hold conferences which enable the generations to congregate and spread their knowledge, and tell others about their own culture as well as learning about others. These conferences are absolutely amazing. There are a great many cultures which have come together to form the Indigenous Youth, stretching from the races of the American Indians, east to the Aborigines in the Australias, and encompassing those in between who hold the same beliefs.

All my experiences combined with the beliefs of my inner self make me the person I am. My name is Karen Chang, the world is a great place and I am proud to be where I am and who I am. Use your wisdom to get the right balance with nature and the human race, and you can reap great rewards of happiness.

Karen Chang was born in 1978 in Kingston Town, Jamaica. She is studying a Foundations of Engineering STEPS course at Brunel University in Uxbridge. She has four half-brothers and eleven half-sisters of whom one brother and six sisters are in Jamaica and the rest in New York. Karen's qualifications are aimed at finding better ways of engineering for the third world. Her ultimate ambition is to achieve a good balance in her life, achieving her own happiness and increasing the happiness in the lives of others.

FEROZE AHMED

Opening Soon

I came to Bristol in 1959 when there were few Pakistani people in the West Country. I had been a student at Oxford Technical College and came to Bristol for business.

Indian food started, as far as this country is concerned, in the early-1950s, but there was no Indian restaurant in the West Country. British ex-army officers who had been in India were more or less the only ones who would eat curries. A few Indian restaurants opened and people realised what they were missing.

I knew there was no Indian restaurant in the whole of the area -- not Weston-super-Mare, nor Bath, nor Bristol, none ... nothing! I wanted to open one in Bristol as I wouldn't face any competition ... still a brave thing to do, but it was a big city, with England's third university and at that time there were about 10,000 full-time students ...

We used to go to London to get the spices every fortnight, or sometimes get them sent by post in a 5lb or 10lb bag. I put a poster in the window -- INDIAN RESTAURANT OPENING SHORTLY -- people used to push the door open, come in and say 'when are you opening? We are longing and waiting for a curry!'

Now after 30 years every corner has a curry house. I wasn't married then, when I opened the first Indian restaurant. I went to Bangladesh where my father arranged the wedding. Then I brought my wife to England in 1961. She was the first Bengali lady in Bristol! She met a Bengali lady in London only after two years ... she was alone 24 hours a day ... there was no chilli, no *paan*, nothing.

Customers were always English, and they still are ... Pakistanis eat at home with their families -- and we didn't open the restaurant for Pakistanis! We opened it for local people. 'Curry and rice' was the most popular food, 'Chicken curry, mixed curry'. People at that time used to think the curries were hot, hot, hot, then we started biryanis. Biryanis are mixed food -- rice and chicken cooked together, dry and we put a small vegetable curry with it. At Stokes Croft, I had one cook to begin with, and now I have six restaurants.

Most of the restaurant owners were not Indian. We used to say 'Indian' food because India, Pakistan, Bangladesh used to be a united India ... so we used to say Indian for business ... at a time like that we used to say we were from India. We didn't mind as India used to be like, say, Great Britain. You don't always say you are from Scotland or Wales ... we used to feel proud that we were Indian, and for the sake of business. At that time Pakistan was only about ten years old. So Indian food meant food from Bangladesh, Punjab, Gujerat, the Sind ... India covered the whole thing.

From my first restaurant I started a Bangladesh Committee in 1971 to support the Bangladeshi Freedom Fighters. The first High Commissioner of Bangladesh came to Bristol -- we invited him to visit. My second restaurant was in the Centre, by the Hippodrome Theatre, called Koh-i-nor. Every night there was a fight. We used to make curry and rice for 3/6d [about 17 pence]-- they used to eat and then they'd run! And we used to catch them! At that time we were young, 18 to 25-year olds. They used to throw rice and curry at each other.

Life has changed. At that time curry was half water and half spice. Now everyone knows curry, what is good, what is bad, now we have cashew nut powder, coconut powder. People know what is good food. When I opened people used to come from as far as Gloucester. Some

people were frightened of curry, but curry doesn't always mean hot, hot, hot. If you like you can have kurma and biryanis. Even children can eat biryanis. We used to use tinned vegetables when we started. Tinned okra! Tinned aubergine! Everything in tins, imported from India. Fresh vegetables only became available in the late-1970s.

Was my coming to England destiny? I don't regret it, it is kismet. England is a rich country compared to Bangladesh ... We have enjoyed living here, we have had a busy life, a chance to earn your living.

When my daughter was born, I felt worried as there were no Bangladeshi families here. I thought she might become a British girl, coming home at midnight when she was only fifteen ... so I decided to take my family back to what was then Pakistan, and I went to the airport, and my son who was only two starting crying 'No Pakistan, no Pakistan!' But we went, and he died there. Did he know, did he see something? He died from a small accident, an unnecessary death. He was left in Pakistan and everyone else is now back in England.

My children think England is their homeland. They have a better life here and better education. All the time, I have tried to start something new. If you start something new there is always potential for things to happen ... I could not finish my studies, I was very weak in English,

but my children have finished theirs. I wanted a good living and to save money to send my children to good private schools -- it cost me a fortune, but I did not smoke, I did not drink or gamble. I sent them to these schools because I was worried at the time about comprehensive education.

When I came to England, I didn't come here to live for ever, for always. I was a student first, and then I started work. When I first came here, I weighed only seven stones, I used to run and play football, nobody could get the ball from me! I didn't know about heart problems, and I used to eat meat three times a day in my curry ... eventually I had a massive heart attack.

I have full respect for England because I have spent 40 years here, but now because I have not been well for twenty years, and have had twenty years of not being active, what can I do? One part of my life has gone -- work. Now I feel that all my children have been educated and can live anywhere in the world, that's OK. But I don't want somebody to insist that I stay in England. My heart is in Bangladesh.

Feroze Ahmed is now retired. Asma, his wife, came to Britain 33 years ago. She works full-time and enjoys sketching and painting in watercolours.

BALJINDER BHOPAL
Three Poems

For My Mother

Made and unmade by you.   Resting
In your curve, wrapped in your prayers
I, the child was born from coal,
Iron and buffalo's milk. Satin
Wrapped itself around you and led
You to my father's house to carry it
Through its roots while we tended it
This season. I grew in your tears'
Flow. In one shone the sun,
The other, rain. You showed
Me your heart, opened in two by migrancy.

Migrant - 1

He is six weeks from Heathrow
The sun is in his skin.
A policeman turns to his scent,
Strange, unknown, beckoning to him.

'Is it Ganja, smack, crack or ecstasy.
Do you buy, sell or smuggle in?'

The two men's faces meet
Continents in between. A van
Comes for this callow man, but
Their cage, it won't hold him in.

Gypsy

I now know the gypsy
In my soul. The baby
Child and her old crone.
Their wander over the globe.
Taking secrets of music
And colour where they go.
And their way, so harsh
And cold. Their songs and
Ghosts, bold. Come back
To India, she wants to rest
Your precious souls.
The Banjaran* calls
Her child must go, but
Their men weep. Gypsy
In my soul, let
The Beloved carry you
On wings wherever
You may go.

* means gypsy in Hindi.

Baljinder Bhopal was born in Glasgow in 1961, the youngest of nine children. She is a solicitor in Bristol, and her husband is a photographer. They have one daughter. Baljinder's interests are poetry, cultural histories, feminism, travel and religions.

ASMA AHMAD

Promises

The dark hole beckoned.
Promises of a better life
In a 'promised land'.
The woolly clouds innocently floated past,
Alluding to future prosperity.
The 'plane quivered with laughter
At the thought of these lost souls
Seeking happiness in new pastures.

وعدے

سیاہ گھمبیر زمین نے بُلایا

بہتر زندگی کے وعدوں کے ساتھ

ایک نئی منزل کی طرف

ہلکے ہلکے بادل گزرے

فریبی خوابوں مسرتوں کو اپنا دکھاتے ہوئے

طوارہ ہنسی کی ساتھ گدگدا اُٹھا

اِن گمراہ مُسافروں پر

جو خُوشیوں کو ڈھونڈ رہے ہیں

نئی راہوں میں

Poetry workshops during the Azaadi Festival, August 1997

NEVILLE E. COPPERSTONE

Home on the Roam

My mother first saw the light of day in Msida, Malta seventy-three years ago, born the fourth of eight children. From her earliest recollections, she resented her Greek mother's strict and often aggressive temperament. But she loved her gentle seafaring father very much.

As a young girl, she too grew to love the sea and often ran across the road from her house to jump into the Mediterranean and enjoy a cool swim. Sometimes her friends dared her to do it. But she often swam across the bay because it annoyed her mother. She knew that a 'Greek slap' awaited her, but it was worth it.

Sometimes, in her quieter moments, my mother forgot about trying to annoy her mother and simply dipped her feet in the water, avidly watching the busy boats, the fishermen and ferries on their daily tasks. She has never been able to forget the shouting talk, the expressive arms, the strong yet exhilarating smell of sea and fish, and those nimble calloused hands of the fishermen repairing their nets.

Her life had never been happier.

A few years later, her mother told her she must enter a convent. So, around 1940, on her sixteenth birthday, my mother entered a convent and as a novice nun spent her time caring for the homeless and the orphaned children.

A short while later, she received a visit from her father who wanted to see her because he was due to sail to the Middle East and had no idea when he would be back. This was the loneliest time of her life.

During the war, my mother became even busier. There were very few quiet moments and very many homeless children. She had little time to reflect on the deep sadness around her. There were daily reports about her family, but little news of her father. Then one day she heard how his ship had been sunk and he was hiding in Alexandria with two other sailors, and that an underground movement was secretly helping them get back to Malta.

Just before the war ended, her father did come home, but he had orders to sail again. So he visited my mother for the last time. Then, as 1947 drew to a close, he died of a heart attack and she had reluctantly to leave the convent to be with her family.

A couple of months later, at the Upper Barracca Gardens, overlooking The Grand Harbour, her mother gave her some news. She has never forgotten the unemotional way her mother told her how a husband had been found for her and that she would be living with his relatives until the wedding.

She innocently asked why.

'Because tomorrow I am leaving for America.'

My mother has never been able to describe her feeling about that meeting. Nor the confused emotions she experienced, never seeing her mother again: the only contact, an occasional letter, photograph and a ten-dollar note at Christmas.

(All I knew about my grandmother was that she had married an American Greek millionaire, she had two of everything and she died just before Christmas around 1990, a year or two after her husband's death. Throughout her life she saw all her children struggle into old age and none of them, not even her natural grandchildren, received a penny from her massive wealth. The entire estate went to the children of her second husband.)

So reluctantly my mother moved in with her prospective husband's family and two months later, in November 1948, they were married; or, rather, Malta's two most influential land and property-owning families married.

Mother thinks of her wedding day as the second saddest moment of her life. And my father did not take long to show his true character. It began on their honeymoon. He condemned drinking but revered gambling and spent many late nights in makeshift clubs.

After the honeymoon they moved into a house belonging to my father's family and, within two months, people were knocking on the door asking for money my father owed them. So they moved to another house owned by the family, and again people started knocking on the door. This time, his family stepped in and paid his debts. And a little while later, in September 1949, I was born.

Even during these difficult times for my mother, my father continued to gamble. They stayed at that house for about two years and then my brother was born. Father grew more frustrated with fatherhood and his gambling became worse. And so we moved yet again to another family home on a different part of the island.

We stayed there long enough for another brother to be born and as the frustrations grew, so did the demands for money. But my father's problems gradually began to get worse. His father died and so did his family's support for his gambling. And once again we were moved on, and on again several more times.

Finally, father suggested that a new country might be the answer to our problems. So in October 1957 we moved to England -- into a draughty sea-front bungalow on Hayling Island. Life was much tougher than any of us expected. We experienced snow, ice and cold for the first time. A frozen sea. And very poor heating.

The weather was frustrating enough for my father, but what angered him more was the lack of work. So for six months we endured the weather, biased and bigoted locals and a strange way of life. Eventually, we returned to Malta. But life had not changed. We moved into a flat in a place called Casal Pawla, then three weeks later we moved into a house in the same place. Everyone was restless and very, very confused. I remember running away from school, just to lie in a field, look at the sun and play with the grasshoppers.

Eventually, mum decided that perhaps England would be the best place for us after all. So she sent my dad ahead to find work and a home. And had her sister, who was already living in Bristol, to help him. He came back to Malta unsuccessful. But undeterred, on August 23rd, 1960, without dad, we moved into a little bedsit in Bishopston with my Aunt Mary and lived in one large room for about nine months.

Eventually, in the spring of 1961, we moved into a council flat in Lawrence Weston in a block which has since been demolished. When dad heard we had somewhere secure to live, he moved back in with us and after some hunting, he found a job at a local shipyard.

By now, I was a teenager and emotionally struggling with the onset of adult life. Several times during this period, I remember coming home, blubbering to my mum how often people had called me a 'bloody foreigner' that day. But new adult responsibilities swifty brought me back to my senses: mother was pregnant again. I had to take charge; as dad was not around, I had to look after my younger brothers. I had just turned thirteen.

A few days after mum came out of hospital, dad informed us he had just been made redundant. But the truth was more surreal. He had not been working at all. So, after a huge row, he left home. A couple of months later -- a few days before Christmas -- we moved into a house in Henbury. Mum remained strong and reliably tolerant. She may have been crying inside, but she never showed us. We had no Christmas presents, no decorations and very little food. I remember being taken into a small room stocked with toys and games belonging to the Toc H charity, and being told to choose one. It was a tough Christmas. We had to put up with prejudiced neighbours. A hard winter. And my adult responsibilities were growing daily. I was now fifteen years old.

Then a few months later, dad turned up again, looking like a tramp. He said he had been living rough. I believed him. For the next couple of years, we tried to live like a 'normal' family, although dad was still out of work. So mum took on two part-time jobs -- one as a cleaner and another as a Peek Freans biscuit packer. And my brothers and I worked in a cramped, humid 6ft x 6ft shed at weekends peeling potatoes for a local chip-shop.

But dad's tempers became more violent, until one day in May 1967 my mum could not tolerate his laziness any further and my father slammed the front door for the last time. None of us saw him again.

Over the years, the neighbours accepted us and one by one we matured, married and left home. My mother now lives very happily a few yards up the road from our last home and she still loves to watch all kinds of seafaring activities. My sister bought that house and is a professional cake maker. One of my brothers half owns and runs a restaurant in France. Another is an assistant branch manager for an international courier service. And the youngest manages a golf club.

Me? I live a couple of streets away from my mum and I write and teach a bit. And dad? Well, he died alone in Malta in the 1980s. He is at peace now, but what makes me sad is that he never saw any of us develop into inspiring adults.

JOSEFA MUNDZIEL

The Journey

My country, my most beloved home
In the year '39 all drenched with blood
It wasn't enough to tear Poland in two
But they had to send us to Siberia too.

February the tenth we won't forget
When the Soviets came, we were still sleeping yet
With our children on sleds they took us away
To the railway station we went that day.

O terrible fear, O terrible hour
Which in torment abandons her dearest to doom;
We'll never forget the moment that came
When they locked us up in a dark wagon-tomb.

So goodbye to the sunshine, the glittering stars
For we're leaving for ever our Fatherland fair;
For four solid days, as we crossed Polish soil,
We said our farewells through the cracks in the wall.

And on the fifth day, a Russian train shrieks
As though each of us there had been stabbed by a sword.
There follow days upon days, there follow weeks upon weeks,
Once a day bread and water they give us on board.

We pass by forests, hills, the Urals
Through the mountains we travel, further and on;
On the fourth of March, as the train clanks still
Another journey begins, against our will.

We trudge forward, pulling our children on sledges
Through mountains, through forests, through taiga and river;
Woeful is our mournful procession,
Getting only boiled water and bread in succession.

The children weep on the sledges, they're chilled to the bone,
They hark back and long for their own dear home.
O Poland most loved, O Poland most holy,
Where are your sons now, your young eagle children?

Half of our people perished in Russia,
The others to Persia eventually broke through;
There they enlisted with the Polish forces
And the world-wide wandering began anew.

JOSEFA MUNDZIEL

10th February 1940

In the year nineteen hundred and forty
The tenth of February was a terrible night,
All through the borderlands of eastern Poland
The silence was shattered by Satanic might.

A horde of Bolshevik ruffians burst
into our houses, our villages, towns,
To snatch the menfolk, the women and children
Those who were fighting for Freedom's crown.

Not even thirty minutes had passed
when on the horses driven in haste
the trembling mothers and children were riding
Headed for barbarous, unknown wastes.

The hearts were hot of the mothers and fathers
They clenched their fists hard, and their palms trickled blood,
Each of them planning a day of vengeance
When their hands would grasp guns and the fight would be good.

Long and hard the journey was
to the utmost north of the USSR,
In filthy wagons, in cold and hunger
Death crept in and took many brothers of ours.

And when at last we heard murmur over our heads
the great firs of the north in a frost-silver coat
We stopped, and into dirty barracks they put us,
our guard a fierce Kommandant, vicious, a brute.

Mockery of the noble Polish
This was our food for a whole long year
Till finally Hitler thwarted their plans
And the Red Star was riven with his iron spear.

Thus came a change in the menacing posture
of the savage Red Lion to its Polish prey,
And then Great Britain came to the rescue
of the brave Poles in slavery, to take them away.

And on August the fifth, at a time towards evening
The dusk was illumined by Freedom's light,
For they declared freedom for all Polish prisoners
And strength most immortal, and hope most bright.

[Translated by **Christina Malkowska Zaba**]

Josefa Mundziel was born in Poland in 1920 and came to England in 1947. She lives in Fishponds, Bristol and enjoys needlework and being a grandmother. She has a son and a daughter, and one grand-daughter. 7

JÓZEFA MUNDZIEL

O naszej podróży

Ojczyzno moja ziemio ukochana
w 39-tym roku cała krwią zalana
Nie dość że Polskę na pół rozerwali
Jeszcze nas Polaków na Sybir wysłali.

Dziesiąty luty będziem pamiętali
Gdy przyszli sowieci myśmy jeszcze spali
I nasze dzieci na sanie wsadzili
I na główną stacje nas odprawili.

O straszna trwoga, o straszna godzina
wzruszająca a bólu swoich zapomina
Ale nam owej nie zapomnieć chwili
Gdy nas w ciemny wagon jak w trumnę wsadzili.

Żegnaj słoneczko i gwiazdy złociste
Bo my odjeżdżamy z ziemi Ojczystej
Całe cztery dni Polskąśmy jechali
Choć my ją tylko przez szpary żegnali.

Piątego dnia sowiecka maszyna ryknęła
Jakby sztyletem każdego przebiła
Mijają doby tygodnie mijają
Raz na dzień wody i chleba nam dają.

Mijamy lasy, góry i urale
A my jedziemy tak daley i dalej
Czwartego marca maszyna ryknęła
I już inny transport się zaczyna.

Idziemy piechotą a dzieci sankami
Górami, lasami, tajgami rzekami
Oj smutna była nasza karawana
Kipiatku i chleba dawali co rana.

Dzieci na sankach zmarznięte płakali
Jeszcze o noclegach naszych pamiętali
O Polsko kochana, o Polsko Ty Święta
Gdzie Twoje syny, gdzie Twoje Orlęta?

Połowa Polaków w Rosii wymarli
A druga połowa do Persii się przedarli
I do Polskiego wojska się pisali
I po całym świecie znów się rozjechali.

JÓZEFA MUNDZIEL

Rok 1940 – 10 luty

W tysiąc dziewięćset czterdziestym roku
Dziesiąty luty była straszna noc
Na całych kresach kochanej Polski
Ciszę rozdarła szatańska moc.

To bolszewicka horda czekistów
Wpadła do naszych osad i gród
By porwać mężów Matki i dzieci
Tych co walczyli o wolny próg.

Nie trwało nawet minut trzydzieści
Kiedy na koniach pędzonych w cwał
Jechały drzące Matki i dzieci
W nieznaną otchłań i dziki świat.

Ojcom i Matkom Krwią serca zaszły
Palce się wbiły, aż do krwi w dłoń
Lecz każdy myślał o dniu odwetu
Gdy się otrzyma w swe ręce broń.

Długa i ciężka ta podróz była
Na daleką północ S.S.S.R.
W brudnych wagonach o chłodzie i głodzie
Wielu z naszych braci znalazła śmierć.

Gdy zaszumiały nam nad głowami
Jodły północne i mrozów szat
Tu nas wsadzono w brudne baraki
I stał nad nami Komendant kat.

Różne szyderstwa na Polskich Panów
To był nasz pokarm przez cały rok
Aż wreszcie Hitler skrzyżował plany
I wbił w czerwoną gwiazdę swój gnot.

Whet się zmieniła grożna podstawa
Lwa czerwonego na Polski łup
Przyszła z pomocą Wielka Brytania
Wyrwać z niewoli dzielny Polski lud.

I w dniu piątego sierpnia wieczorem
Światłem wolności zabłysła noc
Bo ogłoszono Wolność Polakom
Wszak nieśmiertelna była to moc.

MOAZZAM ALI

Passage to England

I was three years old when my father came to England. We were poor but my father was very good at reading the Quoran. Some rich people knew my father very well. So one day, when we were all sleeping, a rich man came to wake my father up. He wanted to take him to England. I was sleeping and I did not know anything about it. That night, my father had to get ready to go to England. He was very happy because he was going to England. He was sad as well because he was leaving his wife, children and his mother behind.

My father is a *maulavi* in a mosque. A maulavi is like a priest. So that is how my father came to England.

When I was six years old I went to play by my house. I saw a man with a beard coming back from the city. He was carrying a lot of fruits in his hand. I ran to the man and grabbed his leg. I thought he was my father but he was another man. My mother saw me grabbing that man's leg, and said, 'he is not your father.'

The man asked where my father lived, and mum said, 'he lives in England, he has not come back yet.' Then the man took out some fruits from his bag and gave them to me.

When I was about eleven years old my uncle got married. We all went to his house. There, I saw all the children playing with their fathers. Some fathers were carrying the children on their shoulders. I said to mum, 'where is father?' She started crying, she missed him very much as well.

A few years later, one day I was playing in a field. Suddenly, I heard that my father was coming back from England after seven years. I had completely forgotten about my father, and I could not remember what he looked like. I saw his photograph with a beard.

When I saw my father there were people all round him. I was really surprised by all these people. Seeing our father after all that time, we felt very happy but there was a question in my head. I said to him, 'why have all these people come to see you?'

My father answered, 'because I am the first person from our village who went to England. The people have never seen a person who has been to England. They don't know what a person from England looks like.'

Next day, my father called us all and gave us a lot of nice presents and clothes. Then he took us all to a big city and we had a great day. We saw many things in the city which we had never seen before. We went to the zoo. He told us to stand by the animals and took our photographs.

One day I bunked off school. I went somewhere else with my friends. Our school finished at 3.30, but I came home at 12 o'clock. My father said, 'where have you been?' I was scared and just stood there and listened to him. He carried on asking questions. I said, 'I did not go to school today.' He asked why not, and then he hit me and said, 'if you ever miss school again I'm not going to let you off. Understand?' I said, 'yes, dad.'

Then a month later, he went back to England. Before he went back, there were questions in his head. He was thinking, 'if my children carry on like this, it will be no good for them.' So my dad went back to England and he took all our photos with him. Two years later, he wrote to tell us he had applied for visas for all of us to come to England. Later we received a letter from Islamabad, telling us to go there to check if we all looked the same as the photographs in our passports.

So, we went to our nan's house. My uncle had a van. We cooked all the food we wanted to take with us, and then went to bed early because we had to get up at about three o'clock in the morning to go to Islamabad. It took us five hours. We went to the embassy, where there was a woman checking all the people. She checked us quickly, and we then joined a long queue. They were calling people inside a room. My grandmother asked, 'how long have we to wait?' She was old and very tired.

In the room there were some white people and some Asian people. The Asian woman asked questions to my father and mother in Urdu. Then four white girls came and talked to us. My brother, two sisters and myself went to another room. I was asked, 'where do you come from, which city, which village? Who do you live with? Your father, your mother, the whole family?' Then they asked who my neighbours were. They carried on asking questions. I answered the questions I understood. Then they asked a question I did not understand. My uncle was there and tried to help, but they stopped him. Then they asked questions to my little brother and older sister. It took a very long time.

A few months later they called us again. This time we went for blood tests. They checked everyone, and they took our mum's blood in front of me and my little brother. He was about nine years old. When he saw mum's blood, he fainted. After the test, we came back from Islamabad and straight to our house.

The following week we all went back to Islamabad again. This time they gave us our passports and we came home. Then after two weeks we got ready to come to England. All our relatives and friends came to see us on the day we left Pakistan. Then we went on a bus to Gujrawala, and from there on a special coach to Islamabad. My cousins and my uncle came with us to say goodbye.

We went to the airport to check in, and then on a bus to go to the plane. My grandmother said, 'is this the plane?' My father started laughing and explained for her. We all got off the bus and onto the plane. We sat down in our seats, me and my two sisters and mum had our seats together. My little brother, my father and my grandmother had their seats together.

They gave us headphones to listen to music. They had a tv on the aeroplane as well. There was a music programme on the tv, then it was dinner time. They gave us some English food. I ate what I liked and left the rest. I was very tired, and went to sleep. When I woke, there was breakfast on the table. After some time the plane landed at Dubai airport. We had twenty minutes to look around. Then we went back to the plane. It took about three hours to come to England. People were waiting for us as we got off. They were my dad's friends. They took us to their house and gave us good meals. We stayed one hour, and then went to our house and had a long sleep.

And this is how we came to be in England.

JANINA SMOLA

Forced Labour

I was born on January 12th, 1925 in Lukowa near Bilgoraj in eastern Poland, one of ten children, five boys and five girls. My parents owned a brick factory and a farm. I was on holiday from school when the Germans invaded Poland on September lst, 1939. I never saw school again. From that time I worked on the farm and in the factory. Times were hard as we were always in fear that we would be arrested or sent to Germany to work camps. The Germans used to set us traps at night, and so the young people would hide in barns or in the hay. Our livestock would be marked and reserved for the Germans, a portion of our crops would be forcibly allocated to them as well. But to feed ourselves we would secretly kill livestock at night and hide the meat.

This continued until June 1943. One day the Germans surrounded the whole village because they said partisans were hiding in the woods and some must have come from our village. Also, the partisans had stolen some of the allocated livestock, chopped off the ear with the ring which signified this was cattle allocated to the Germans and sent it to the town hall. They also blew up German installations and bridges. Because of this, we were all arrested, loaded onto lorries and sent to Zwierzyniec, a temporary German camp. After a few days we were loaded into cattle trucks at the railway station and sent to Majdanek, a German prison. There were many Jews there. On the first day, we were herded into what looked like a stable, no windows, and straw, water and manure on the floor. There were so many of us we couldn't move. People were fainting with thirst and lack of air. It was raining that day and we noticed water coming through the roof. People stood on each other's shoulders to get a cup of water which they passed round.

In the morning the belongings we had brought with us were taken away. They sent us to a bath-house where we had to strip off our clothes, the women had to put on trousers, tunic tops and caps. They then separated my father and brother. I was left with my mother, sister-in-law, her child, my youngest brother and three sisters.

We were sent to a barrack where there were about 400 of us. At 4 o'clock each morning we had to quickly leave the barrack and line up outside in fours while the Germans did a head count. There we stayed until four in the afternoon. Our beds were double bunks made from planks of wood. Fleas abounded, I remember my mother removing my youngest brother's trousers and slapping them on a stone to kill the fleas. In the barrack there was a trough which we had to use as a toilet and, with the number of people there, it soon overflowed onto the barrack floor. For breakfast we were given black coffee and a thin slice of bread. Lunch was soup made from I don't know what, but there were more stones and sand than vegetables. I can't remember if we had anything later in the day but I do remember we used to save mouldy crumbs which were mixed with the coffee and given to my brother as extra food because he cried with hunger. This was how we lived for the next five weeks.

One day the Germans announced over the tannoy that certain families would be sent to work camps in Austria. My family was one of these. The next day our belongings were returned to us, we put on our clothes, and were loaded onto lorries and taken to a camp near Lublin, where they had to feed us up a bit so that we could work. Many people were sick because of this extra food, not having eaten properly for so long. My sister was one of these. We were in this camp for two days and then marched about three kilometres to a railway station, loaded onto wagons and sent to a prisoner-of-war camp in Gratz, Austria. There we were sent to a shower house, where we stripped off and had our first proper wash since being arrested. Some women came and washed our hair with paraffin to remove the fleas. My sister was taken to the camp hospital, then removed to a proper hospital as she was seriously ill.

In this camp conditions were better; we were kept clean and the food was slightly better. I can't remember how long we stayed, but one day some farmers came and picked us out to work on their farms. One farmer picked my parents, myself, one older brother and one younger brother and my two younger sisters, the third was still in hospital. My other brother and sister-in-law were taken by a different farmer. We were a long way from each other.

Although the work was hard, I shared a bedroom with a German woman and had enough food, but my parents and the other children were sleeping in a barn on straw. My parents were ill-treated by the farmer's wife, who beat them with a broom. I worried how to help them and one day a friend of the farmer came to visit him and noticed how hard-working I was. His wife was in hospital and he went to an office similar to a labour exchange and asked if he could take me to work for him. The office agreed, and he came to our farmer with the letter. My farmer refused to let me go, threatening to shoot me if I tried to leave. I had picked up some German, and whispered that I would escape that night. After finishing my work I usually met up with my brother and we would sit around and talk. That night, I had already packed my meagre belongings and had them with me. The farmer and his wife had gone to bed; Farmer 2's labourer had come for me and was waiting. In the meantime, my room-mate returned to the bedroom, noticed my empty bed and my missing belongings. She woke the farmer, who ran out shouting

and firing his gun. My brother ran to a nearby wood, the labourer ran home and I ran into a potato field and on hands and knees crept along until I was out of sight. Farmer 1 thought my brother had taken me and was shouting for him to come back.

My poor parents suffered a beating and the farmer wanted to throw them off the farm. My father said he would go in the morning. Eveything quietened down, and my parents fell asleep in the barn. I was still in the potato field wondering what to do. I crept to the barn and woke my parents and told them not to let me sleep. I would creep away just before daybreak, but I fell asleep on the hay and woke to hear the farmer calling my parents. I hid in the hay and the youngest children lay on top of me, while he searched in the hay but luckily he just missed me.

My parents went to work and I waited until everyone went for their breakfast. I then crept out of the barn into the potato field, crawled until I was out of sight and ran to the next farm where I was told that Farmer 2 lived just across the field. I ran to his farm, he gave me breakfast and told me my duties. The next day I was stacking wood when he came and told me to hide as my former employer was coming with my family. I hid under his bed. Farmer 1 said he was only keeping my family because of me and didn't want them any more. Farmer 2 explained he only had permission to take me, but my family stayed with him anyway. They were fed and sent to the office where there was a very nice German lady, who after my father's explanation gave him a letter to take to Farmer 1 saying he had to keep them. In the meantime, she would try to get them sent home. In a week or two my family returned home but I had to stay and work.

I worked on this farm until the war ended in 1945. Work was hard but at least I had enough to eat. Following the German capitulation, the American and Polish army told all the workers to collect at a camp and from there we were taken to Italy to Polish camps with the Polish army. There I met my husband.

In the autumn of 1946 I came to England to Hillingbury in Southampton. There I stayed for about three weeks, then moved to a Polish army camp in Malmesbury for about three months, where I was reunited with my husband, and then to Stowell Park near Cirencester. In 1948 he was demobilised and we moved to Northwick Park, Evesham where he worked. While there, we heard there was housing and work in Bristol, and so we moved to the camp at Lulsgate just outside the city. In 1963 we moved to our present home here, where we have lived for 35 years.

THEO and NORMA SOBERS
Deep Freeze, New Family

Theo and Norma Sobers live in Bath and have been married for 33 years. They both come from Barbados, and were friends there before emigrating to Britain. Theo came here in 1960, and Norma followed two years later. They married in 1964 at Walcot Church, Bath. They talk with Shawn Naphtali about their life together since then.

So what made you come to England in the first place?

Theo: I think I was influenced by friends, really. Most of my friends were leaving, and my best friend at the time encouraged me to come over.

Why was everyone coming to England?

Theo: At the time, we were told the job prospects were good. I think a lot of people wanted to take the chance and see what it was really like. I wanted to see for myself.

What sort of work were you looking for?

Theo: Oh, I don't think you had that in mind, it was just work to get money. The type of work was not the priority.

How did your family take it?

Theo: They encouraged me as well, but at the same time they didn't want to see me go.

You've been here for 37 years. Did you always plan to stay so long?

Theo: For most of us, including myself, the plan was five years. Back then, five years was a long time. Ten at the very most. Did we plan to stay indefinitely? No.

And what made you come over? *(addressing Mrs Sobers)*

Norma: Well, like he said, friends were leaving. You just wanted to see another part of the world and earn some money. And my sister came over, she was my only sister, and we'd always done the same things. Little Sister wants to do the same as Big Sister.

Were you looking for a particular type of job?

Norma: No, not particularly. I just thought whatever job came along I would be willing to have a try. My first job was at a geriatric nursing home in Leicester, doing auxiliary nursing at the time.

Did you have the same five-year plan, or did you plan to stay longer because of your sister?

Norma: Well, no one thought they would be away from their family for thirty-odd years. We all thought we would come for a short stay and then return. But five years turned into ten, ten into twenty and now it's over thirty.

Did you travel to England alone?

Norma: Yes. I knew no one else on the flight, but I got talking to other passengers and by the time we landed we were like a close family because for everybody, it was their first time leaving home.

How old were you then?

Norma: That would be giving my age away a bit, wouldn't it! Well, I had just turned 21, because in those days you had to be 21 before you could sign documents. My birthday was in March, and right after that my dad helped me pay for my flight. I was met at Gatwick Airport by my cousin, and I was quite amazed. I kept looking out for the nice houses and pretty gardens which I thought England would be full of, but all I could see as we travelled was the back of houses and little chimneys on top. I wondered if they were a whole lot of little factories, because in Barbados, the only time you saw a chimney poking up into the sky was on top of a factory which was grinding sugar canes, you know, or engineering work.

How long was it before you first contacted each other again in England?

Norma: Theo knew I was coming over, and he came to London to meet me in a matter of days, actually. I was staying with relatives. He came back to Bath and I went to Leicester to my sister who was doing her nurse training and he used to visit me there. When my sister finished her training and decided to leave, that's when I came over to Bath.

Theo, what kind of work were you doing at the time?

Theo: Engineering, just as now.

What drew you to Bath in the first place?

Theo: I lost my job in London. I decided to come to Bath visiting family for a weekend, and happened to get a job, so I came here to live.

How did you lose your job in London?

Theo: According to the foreman, I was late back at work, but I didn't think I was. It's fair to say he didn't like me very much, always used to pick on me, reasons unknown. I think that was the best chance he had of getting rid of me. There was no union or anyone to complain to, so it was just his word against yours. He took me to the guv'nor and said I was late, and according to him I had no intention of make any excuses or whatever. So the guv'nor said, 'if you can't get on, one of you has to go!', and it was obvious it had to be me. I wasn't going to say sorry for something I didn't do. That's about it.

Was it hard for black people to get jobs at that time?

Theo: At the time I would say no, especially where I was. I must admit, though, they used to employ a lot of black people because we were seen as cheap labour. I would say at least 90 per cent of the workforce there was black. After I lost that job, though, I couldn't get another straightaway, and I didn't want to sign on the dole, and my money was running out. And that's when I got the job in Bath. The funny thing is that as soon as I settled in Bath, my mate in

London forwarded my post. It turned out I was accepted for most of the jobs I had applied for in London, but by then it was too late for the interviews.

Norma, you mentioned working in hospitals. I've noticed a lot of West Indian women work in hospitals. Why do you think that is?

Norma: Well, when we came over to England first, I think we liked caring a lot and it was quite easy to get work in hospitals. It was a job, and we all thought it was a nice thing, and you like to know you're doing something to help people, and you just stick at it.

What sort of jobs did the black men find they were doing?

Theo: They took up with London Transport in the early days. It was more secure. Actually, it was they who started a lot of the migration to England -- they came over to Barbados in the mid-1950s to recruit people to work on the buses. Other companies came over and recruited people to work in hotels, nursing and also in textiles. It was recruitment, and the reason black people took them [the jobs] was because it was secure -- not only a secure job, but accommodation as well. Even before leaving Barbados, we had to sit exams and have blood tests and everything. They were making sure you were educated and healthy before you came to England.

Do you ever wonder what it would have been like if you had both stayed in Barbados?

Theo: Well, yes sometimes, of course you do think back, but you will never know the answer. I can't say I have ever regretted it. There were times, when things weren't going too well, and as I said, most of us came here saying it would be for five, ten years at the most. But then you get commitments, and ten years have passed before you even think about it! That's how most of us have got stuck here ... but I wouldn't say I have any regrets. I know that a lot of people who stayed in Barbados are now doing very well, very well indeed. As a matter of fact, I would say better than many of us over here.

Did you keep good contact with your family in Barbados after you came over?

Norma: Oh yes, we never lose contact with family! Always wrote very often and was always promising to go back, but once you have children, it's not always that easy. The first time I went back was in 1972 with my two little children, but it was lovely! Seeing old school friends, mum and dad, aunts and uncles. It was lovely.

Theo: I always kept in contact with my family and wrote every week, but it was fifteen years before I went back on my first visit. I could have gone before, but I'm not a great lover of travelling, so regretfully, I left it as long as possible. It was nice when I first got back and I wondered why I had left it so long -- everyone was glad to see me, more than glad! Familiar faces, new faces, additions to families you never knew before -- it was great.

How do you feel whenever you go back now? Do you still feel a part of that culture or slightly removed from it?

Theo: In some ways, you've been living in another country for so long you find you have different habits and your culture fades a bit. I'm not saying it completely goes, but you've got to say you change a bit -- living in another country for more than half your life. Once you get back to Barbados, though, it doesn't

take long for your birth culture to come back.

Norma: It feels as if you're thawing out of a deep freeze. You don't have time to get used to it, though, because work will only let you have a certain amount of time off, and it's never enough. When you get back, you feel you need another holiday to get over the one you've just had! Once you're over there, though, you get into a few sea baths and you feel really happy.

So are you planning to go back there to live?

Norma: Well, we all have our dreams. I would like to go back to live some time. My dad died four years ago, my mum is at home. My sister lived in America for quite a few years but she's gone back to Barbados to live now. She's got her own house and so has my mum, but at the moment there's no great push. I'm looking forward to going back some time. We've got property over there at the moment which is being built. It'll probably be finished by the end of the year. When we go over and see it for the first time, we probably won't want to come back. With God's help, we would like to return to Barbados some time.

Theo: I've still got a few years more left before retirement, so I'd like to see that through, but hopefully, hopefully, some time, yes ...

WACLAW DOMAGALA
Life in a Soviet Camp

I was born on January 24th, 1924 in a town called Miechow in southern Poland. My parents owned a farm and I was the youngest of seven children. In 1937 my family moved to Kolonia Podlipie, twelve kilometres from Zloczow in south-eastern Poland, where we continued to work our own farm.

On September 1st, 1939 the German army invaded Poland from the west and seventeen days later, the Russian army crossed our eastern borders. Life became extremely difficult. We were constantly attacked by Ukranian gangs who murdered and set fire to neighbouring farms.

On February 10th, 1940 at six o'clock in the morning there was a knock at the door. A Russian officer and two soldiers were on the doorstep. They were taking us to the railway station in Zloczow. We packed what we could, mainly food and clothes, and were then escorted by sleigh to Zloczow station. We were loaded into cattle wagons, packed so tight that we had to take it in turns to sleep. While some stood, others slept. The windows were boarded up, doors locked, the toilet was a hole in the floor with a funnel. We waited like this until each wagon was full, in temperatures of -40 degrees centigrade. When the train was ready, we departed for an unknown destination.

Our journey lasted about three weeks. During this time the train would stop to allow everyone to relieve themselves by squatting either side of the train under guard and to allow designated people to collect soup and *kipiatok* (boiling water from the locomotive) for each wagon. Our destination was still unknown. During the journey, those who weren't strong enough died and their bodies were thrown out by the soldiers. Pregnant women were taken off, not to be seen again. At last the train

stopped, the station was Kirow in Komi S.S.R. We were told to get off the train and were loaded into lorries which travelled 150 kilometres to a place called Noszul; there, sleighs were waiting, our luggage, children and the elderly were loaded on and we then set off on foot across a frozen river (Luza) for 72 kilometres. We arrived at camp number 3 where we divided in half, and my family and the group I was with continued for a further six kilometres.

On arrival there were two barracks of living accommodation, a kitchen and a recreation hall. Each barrack consisted of four rooms and six families were allocated to each room. Beds were made of planks, there was a stove at one end of the room, bedding was what you had brought with you. This was to be our home for the next 18 months. In winter it was bearable but in summer we were plagued by mosquitoes and bugs which dropped from the ceiling and crawled out from the walls and beds and sucked the blood.

Next day, the commandant came and allocated our work. On this day my grandfather died as a result of the hardship he had suffered on the journey. We had to bury him ourselves in the frozen ground. My job at the camp was to cut and burn the branches off the trees which the adults had cut down and to remove the bark. We worked from six in the morning until six at night, and were supposed to be paid but the money never materialised. Instead, we were given food. If you reached your quota you received a kilo of bread; for those who didn't work, the quota was 300 grammes of bread a day. The workers' quota was impossible to attain, so we found ways of beating the system in order to survive. Once the controller had measured your work, he marked it with a stamp; when he left we sawed the marked piece away and got the wood ready for the next day, thus ensuring our kilo of bread.

One day, as I was returning to camp after work, I was starving and spotting a field of potatoes decided to dig some out and fill my pockets. The commandant saw me and took me to the police, where they wrote out a two-page statement saying I had stolen State-owned potatoes. I was brought before a court of three judges, but because I was under-age I was released. This was our existence, we supplemented our diet with wild mushrooms and berries. I suffered from a condition known as 'chicken blindness' (night blindness caused by lack of vitamins and minerals). I saw nothing from dusk until dawn. During this time, my mother died of severe stomach pains and my brother drowned while helping make a log dam across the river.

Someone had a radio hidden which they listened to at night and we learned that Germany had attacked Russia. The Russian army was weak at this time and the Polish government in exile seized the opportunity to sign a pact with Stalin to release the Polish prisoners-of-war and the deported civilian population, and to form a Polish army in the U.S.S.R.

Stalin gave the Poles an 'amnesty' which enabled them to leave the camps. In October 1941 my father, sister and I, along with three other families, decided to go in search of the Polish army. We made a raft, loaded what was left of our belongings and made our way back to Noszul. There, we exchanged the raft for lodgings until the snow fell, as we were to travel by sleigh. When the snow came, we made little sledges for our belongings and set off on foot for Kirow. Before we left Noszul, my father spotted a truck and discovered that they had brought goods from Kirow. He asked the driver if he could take us there. The driver replied that he had been instructed not to assist any Polish people, but if we went out of town, he would pick us up and take us as far as he could. This we did, and he dropped us on the outskirts of town. We went to the railway station and found a train with prisoners-of-war

from Kotlas. Their train was full, but they told us to head south where the Polish army was forming.

My father and the other men went to the station-master and explained the situation. He assigned a wagon to us and we had to wait for the next transport to come along, approximately a week later. When the train arrived, our wagon was attached and we were on our way. Our journey consisted of shuntings and sidings, waiting for trains, looking for food until the next stop. On one of the food forays, my father and a friend were left behind and I never saw him again. Later, in Teheran, I found that my father had died of typhoid.

I was left with my sister and one pair of boots between us. During our journey, my sister, too, got left behind looking for food. Luckily she was able to get on a train carrying Russian children evacuated from Moscow and at one of the stations, this train and mine were stationary side-by-side. I asked a man from our wagon, as I had no shoes, to see if my sister was on that train. He found her, and so we were reunited.

At one of the stations we met a Polish military delegation who were recruiting for the army and I joined up. I had to go to Saratow which I reached in December and then to Tatishczewo where the 5th Division was quartered. There I was enlisted as an Army cadet. Sometime later, in 1942, I was reunited with my sister and we left together for Krosnovlodsk port. We were transported by ship to Pahlevi in Persia and here I said goodbye to my sister. She was eventually evacuated to East Africa and I stayed in the army camp.

Here I contracted malaria and when I recovered I rejoined my unit in Iraq. I fought with the 2nd Corps, survived the Battle of Monte Cassino in Italy, but was wounded in Ancona in July 1944 (for which I received Poland's highest military cross, *Virtuti Militari*) and following the amputation of my left leg was transported by ship to England, to the Polish hospital in Ormskirk where

I arrived in October 1944. From that date until May 5th, 1948 when I was demobilised, I spent my time in hospitals, convalescent and rehabilitation homes. While I was in the rehabilitation home near Newton Abbot, an officer from the labour exchange came and recruited Polish men to work in Bristol in the recently opened Remploy factory.

I met and married my wife in Southampton in 1949 and we settled in Bristol where I live to this day.

KRYSTYNA STUDZINSKA-TRIBEDI
Poland to Bristol

I came to live in Bristol in 1987. I chose Bristol because my only child married a Bristol girl and settled here, and I now have two grandchildren.

I was born in Poland in 1937. When the war broke out I was nearly two. My father was in the Polish army which withdrew from Poland when the Germans attacked without warning. I am not sure whether my father was in Hungary or in Rumania. The Poles hoped that their allies would rally round to repel the Germans, but that did not happen. I know my father was in France when it fell to the Germans and to escape he got on a ship thinking he was sailing to America. Instead, he landed in Scotland where he remained. He was a doctor and worked in the military hospital in Taymouth Castle, Perthshire and lodged in Aberfeldy, the 'heart of Scotland'. My father did not know what was happening to us, nor we to him, till 1946.

In Poland, we were thrown out of our house, packed into a cattle train, and taken to another part of the country. People of the town took us into their homes and later we went to live in the village where my father had been born and where his mother lived. We stayed in a wooden cottage with no water, no electricity and an outside lavatory. But to me it was all an adventure. The war came to our village and we ran away. It was still all an adventure to a child, as long as no one died. But my grandfather died -- in Auschwitz concentration camp -- because he was educated, a lawyer.

After the war we settled in Silesia and managed to trace my father, who organised our escape from communist Poland. We came to Glasgow in 1947, where I met and married a Bengali. For some time we lived in Calcutta, but decided to return to Britain.

Krystyna is 60 and has been in Bristol for ten years. Originally a biochemist she switched to teaching, became a Principal Teacher of Chemistry, and is now retired but works as a voluntary counsellor for 'Life' Pregnancy Care Centre. Her husband was Bengali, and died in 1996. She has one son who is half-Indian and half-Polish, but born in Scotland, and two grandchildren. She keeps in touch with family in America (her brother's family), often visits family in Poland and is soon to visit her Indian family.

CARMEN ALFONSO
Dis-placements

(A Nils, companero de viaje)

1. Over here (in English)

Telephone rings.

Hello, can I help you?
(with an accent that has been identified many times as being French, German or Scottish)

Could I speak with .... please?

Can you spell the surname for me please?

(Repeats the full name louder)

Please could you spell the surname?

(Sighs and spells the full name very, very quickly)

I am sorry but I didn't catch that.

You idiot. Can't you speak English? Click.

Hello?

2. Over there (in Spanish and with much love)

My God, you are so pale. You look like a cheese. One of those white, white cheeses. A mozzarella cheese, for example. You look ill. Have you been ill lately? Does the sun ever come out in that island? I think not. Probably not. Go on, open the window and stick your head out. You'll see. You'll get back your original colour in no time. You are also thin. I'm sure you've lost weight. Yes you have. What do you eat exactly? No meat? The mad cows? Never heard of them. Don't worry, I've been cooking ... we'll get meat around those bones again very quickly. Now, has someone died in the last week? I thought not. You are too young to be dressed like a widow. Black is only for old ladies and nuns. I think red suits you. There you go, try it on. It's your size. You look lovely. Something is missing, though. Oh yes, you need lipstick. Believe me, it will help. And also, put this on your cheesy cheeks ... you see? Was your hair always so straight?

3. In between (thanks to the Royal Mail)

Waiting for the envelope, long and white, with red stripes on the borders, with the blue, recognisable calligraphy, the Amazonian jungle stamps, the incorrect or incomplete post code, the name of the street wrongly spelt. Clinging to the promise, to those words that she has 'already sent' so many times. And that I have already answered, in advance. Just in case.

Carmen Alfonso is a Spanish teacher and translator. She was born in Bogota, and arrived in England in 1990. She is currently doing research about Colombia in the nineteenth century, studying watercolours, maps and travel writing during this period.

I knew nothing about England before I came. My son applied for me. I could not think of anything ... I was already 63 at that time. Who would employ me, an old woman.... I felt strange. It's only June but the wind was rattling the trees and the leaves were falling ... I wondered why England was so cold.

... When I arrived at the airport, I saw someone who had long hair but this person was wearing a tie as well! I looked at this person at the back, it seemed she was a woman. But when I looked from the front, it seemed she was not a woman, because she was wearing a tie. I just stared at the person. I thought he neither looked like a man nor a woman. Then I thought, he could be a man, because he's wearing a tie.

... I found the houses in England were very neat and tidy ... the houses in my village in China were not that practical ... they're so small, there's no partition. The houses here in England have a pattern, a style, say... a garden. My house in China looked like a box and the roof was flat so that we could dry our clothes there.

... A seaman who had been to England before told me that in England, they had vehicles running on the roofs of the houses! I didn't understand, but when I came I did understand. He meant bridges built over the houses. That's true! The vehicles were running on the roofs of the houses. Like the arches in Gloucester Road, the railway line runs above the houses.

MARGARET GRIEW

50 Years After

They came to remember
to that place that was their hell
in the January chill
clothed now but still frozen
wearing again tatters of blue and white
ironically matching their flag
lighting candles,
wailing their prayers for the dead --
our dead.

'Close your eyes, my friends'
we were exhorted
but we needed no imagination
just the reality of this stark and bestial place:
bed planks and ovens,
railway lines, the mocking
'Arbeit macht frei' --
would that it could.

Sitting in the warmth of home
hearts touched and in pain
silently we sat, frozen,
guilty in survival
we who have not suffered.

Margaret Griew was born in London in 1932 and attended North London Collegiate School. She is married with a grown-up son and daughter. She moved with her family to Bristol in 1960. In middle-age she trained as a social worker at Bristol University. Now retired, she does voluntary work and writes poetry.

What is to be, is to be! My destiny ...

'No, never! I would love to go for the holidays, but not to live there ...' was my answer to friends and family. I had been to Britain in 1965 for studies and lived in London for a year. I knew the weather for a start and the free society life-style. I did not like it a lot ... but maybe it was because of the way I was brought up.

While I was in Britain, I had not visited Bristol. Later in 1967 I got married to a man who would want to live only in Britain. What was I supposed to do? I had to come to Bristol. When I left Kenya on November 1st, 1967, I did not know what my life would be like. I knew I had to make married life happy and build a home in a new environment on British soil. It was different to come as a student and it was surely going to be very different to be wife to a man you knew for only a month. It seemed we would have a shop and I would be behind a counter all my life. Divine powers had something else planned for me.

As I boarded the plane I wondered what would happen to my identity, my way of life and my religion. The feelings were mixed, and there were no answers. I had a sister in Kent and other relations, but they seemed too far away. Everyone was busy. I was leaving behind a life that had been carefree and so happy. What would be the expectations of the new society -- and my husband? And what of his friends? Would I need to change my dress? (In fact, as things turned out, I have always worn my saree, and was the first woman in the United Kingdom to wear it to work, at Marks and Spencer in Bristol!) What of my diet? What would my neighbours be like? And, most profoundly, how would I bring up any family I might have -- could they keep our culture and their roots?

When I arrived in Bristol, I had to share a flat before we bought a house. I was on my own when my husband went to work. Immediately, I tried to find out if there were any Asians or some sort of organisation for us in Bristol. There was an Indian Association, but not many members. To start with there were very few families settled in the area. Of Asians, there were hardly four Gujerati families. So, I began networking! When we had our home I invited families to a regular gathering, so we could retain our culture and traditions, especially our mother tongue. We used to enjoy this very much. Everyone would bring a dish ... we would sing *Bhajans*, talk, tell jokes, and we decided to meet every fortnight and take it in turns to host it. I had set up a shrine and a library in my house which people made use of. Everything began to fall into place, and the worry of being lost was almost gone. For the very first time I had managed to organise an Indian folk dance for the St Paul's Carnival.

By now I felt stronger and able to work. I had taken up office work, but wasn't happy with it. I never wanted to work in a launderette or a factory. I had gone through discrimination and racism but at the time I had not recognised it. I was brought up with the philosophy of equality and giving opportunities to everybody who had the required skills. So I did not notice. My husband is a pharmacist. He has given me great support, without which I would not have achieved any of the things in my life.

I had my first son in 1972, the second two years later. Raising a family was hard. Luckily I had very good neighbours. They were not all like that, we had to win some over ... They were very frightened to have different people living in their neighbourhood. However, there were some who had lived in India during the British Raj who wanted to share their experiences with us.

Because of all this, I came to feel that cross-cultural learning was very important if we all had to live happily together. I began some voluntary work to share my way of life, culture and religion with people -- in schools and with the Women's Institute. As my children grew older, I found it so much more difficult to retain my culture and traditions and my language. There was no provision for this at all, but at the time Asian vegetarian cooking was my main interest and I started to do it for fund-raising -- I helped schools with my expertise in Indian cooking! Ingredients were difficult to find in the early days but as more Asian people began settling in Bristol it became easier and easier.

As time went by, I began teaching in Adult Education and then expanded to consultancy and voluntary work. At the moment, it seems as if I have always lived in Bristol. There are a great many difficulties and every day is another challenge: racism and discrimination seem to have grown. I don't know whether it was hidden then and is open today.

But I feel I have been lucky -- with people and their kindness, understanding and accepting me with respect as I am. One learns from one's mistakes, and I have learned a great deal over the years! My hard work has been recognised by the country and the Queen awarding me an MBE. I have also been awarded the International Mother India Award: Delhi 1993. I was nominated for Woman of the Year in 1990. I believe everything has two sides. One needs to learn to look at the positive side and make the most of the negative -- take those challenges and become strong. I know many people who have really gone through a hard time, especially when I was working with the Uganda Asian Expulsion Committee.

It was thirty years in November 1997 that I came to Bristol. I have no regrets. I like Bristol very much and it is a growing city with much to offer. Who gets used to the weather? But remember your roots and your origins -- it's the greatest wealth anybody can have.

Yashu Amlani MBE is married to a pharmacist and has two children. She has been very involved in voluntary work which aims to promote cross-cultural education. She is also an adult education tutor and set up the Raj Vidya Vihar Saturday Schools for Asian women and children. She enjoys writing, travelling, sports and walking.

KHURSHEED THAJDIN

A Long Trauma

He tripped over my feet as I was sitting down on the floor, my legs stretched out. There was a deep cut on his tongue, bleeding. My husband panicked. It had been a long struggle for my little boy, aged two years, puffy eyes, swollen body and his belly extended. He had just been under medication in the hospital at Kampala.

All of a sudden, we had to leave Uganda for an unseen destination. It was the time of Idi Amin, the president of Uganda. All non-Africans were ordered to leave their homes, businesses and belongings. It was a time of turmoil, and a hell we did not deserve.

We stayed at my sister-in-law's place during our last few days in Uganda. My grandmother, parents, uncle, brothers and sister came from Jinja, sixty miles from Kampala, and boarded a plane in Entebbe. My husband, mother-in-law, my son and I left Masindi to be in Kampala for the flight to England from Entebbe. With other families, we hired taxis to get there, and had some escorts from the military to get to Kampala safely. The escorts were good friends of the family. On the way to Kampala we faced a number of humiliations. We were stopped several times by armed troops. They ordered us out of the taxis, dragged off our luggage, searched and took whatever they wanted. We had only £50 a family and a few clothes. We had to leave everything behind.

The armed men pointed their rifles at us, a shot was fired but missed. They shot other people in the legs. They tortured others. The husband of one of my tutors was tortured and then murdered, and at the end no one was allowed to see his body. He was buried under pointed rifles. Some families were tortured in their own homes. My husband had to run for a shelter when some so-called military troops targetted him. He ran for his life to Masindi. He told me this long after it had happened.

We were still there, being checked; people were trying to be nice to them, the 'authorities'. Eventually it was "kwaheri" and we left. Shaken, grateful for our lives.

We stayed with other relatives in a big flat and as their flight dates approached, they said goodbye and left to an unknown destination and an unknown future. It was like going through a black hole, or waiting for your turn for Doomsday, waiting to see if it would be hell or heaven at the end.

It was there that my son tripped over my feet and was bleeding. My mind was totally occupied with his illness. Everything else seemed to be a vivid dream or a nightmare. I can remember hardly anything of the plane journey. I can only recall a flood of people at Entebbe Airport waiting to fly off from their nest for ever; for many, never to come back, leaving their homes and possessions, their pasts and their dreams.

I can barely remember being searched. They did this as if we were taking the soil of Uganda with us and leaving nothing for them to put their feet on. I remember scarcely anything of the flight. Quite a few people later, in England, asked if I could remember them, as we had met on board. I just said yes, not wanting to offend them.

As we got off the plane, a camera crew was there. The Ambassador to Uganda was returning to England on the same flight. It was a cold winter night, wet and windy. We were guided to the sitting area of the airport. The staff were very helpful and were dishing out winter coats to keep us warm. I was taken straight to the medical unit with my son. They appeared to have been notified about his illness. He was supposed to have gone to the hospital from there. We went with other relatives to a hostel in London, where we were given a hot meal and a bed for the night.

Next morning, my husband and I took my son to hospital in the taxi which was provided for us. That day, we were supposed to leave the hostel and go to a camp, but we waited because of my son. Eventually we settled near Minehead. Most of my family went to other places in England, and I was left with my mother-in-law and my husband, who had a job at the camp. For most of this time, my mind was totally occupied by my son's illness and nothing else interested me. When I try to remember those days, I just get glimpses of the missing time, as I cannot recall much.

I went with my son to the Dorchester Children's Hospital, and from there he went to a hospital in Taunton. During this period my grandfather died in Birmingham, but I was in no position to attend the funeral. Meanwhile, my son was getting worse,and the doctors decided to send him to Guy's Hospital in London. Somehow, he was moved instead to the Bristol Children's Hospital and would have left without me had I not been there. It was sheer luck I got there in time. Without all the medical files, the doctors there could not diagnose his illness and gave him medication to which he reacted badly. The files had been sent to London. After all my sleepless nights I was in a daze -- I couldn't even begin to ask questions.

My son got worse, and there was panic. My family visited. My husband came, along with nursing staff from the camp. I felt I was losing my senses. I was told to pray as the medication was not working. After a few days of hell, he started to get better. My son had never been a 'cry baby' but he had gone through so much suffering, and now he wouldn't leave my side. At the camp, my husband was asked to transfer to Scotland, where the accommodation was miles from any sort of public transport -- a remote village where the buses ran only four times a day. Our camp nurse was angry about this, and successfully fought our case for us not to move to Scotland. She managed to find accommodation for us in Bristol, staying with a couple. My husband moved there, and I stayed at the hospital with my son. Later I moved out, staying days in the hospital and nights at our temporary home in the city.

Gradually, my son improved and was allowed home over weekends, and then for short breaks. In Bristol, I had a visitor; she was a Hindu and I am a Muslim. She asked if we would mind her visiting us? She did visit, and over time we have become very close, as close as family.

My son is now cured. It was, as they said, a miracle that he survived his failing kidneys. I nearly lost him. During this time, I also lost my dear grandmother, which broke me even more. Later I was to lose a lot of relatives, one after the other. I was allotted a large bundle of woes. With my son, even now if he just sneezes, I start to worry. But coming to Bristol from Uganda probably benefitted me. Although my son was on similar medication there, he was looked after very well here in Bristol.

It took me a long time to wake up to England, and after years I still suffer from the trauma of exodus. But I realise I have travelled a long way from Uganda -- more than most people ever have to, to conquer Life's destiny.

Khursheed Thajdin is married with two grown-up children. She comes from Uganda, brought up in Jinja and married in Masindi. She likes writing, cooking, crafts, reading and loves travelling.

If You Can Live in Bristol

I arrived in Bristol in 1956, on October 31st, to be precise. I went to work in a mental hospital. The hospital was then called Fishponds Mental Hospital -- it has since changed to Glenside Health Trust, Blackberry Hill. I was then Esther Layne and met my husband while living here.

Well, the reason for my being in England was that there was no work in my country of origin, which is Barbados. So when I had the opportunity of coming to England I made the move. We as children were always taught that England was our Mother Country so I had the chance to see for myself ...

Well, I can say that Bristol was a very tough place to settle in. One always got remarks such as 'why don't you get back up the trees and go back to where you came from', doors shut in your face when looking for accommodation and as soon as they saw you were a black person. Then when you did get a room to live in there was no bath, so one had to go to a bath-house to get a bath. There was also no heating, so one had to heat the room by means of paraffin heaters, and one did not get used to the cold. It was very difficult to get warm. Also, one had to share the same kitchen with other tenants. There could be as many as six people living in one house.

Even now one still gets remarks after all these years ... one could go on to write a great deal more about Bristol.

Anyway, I am now settled with a husband and four daughters and two grandchildren. It was missing my home, family and friends and such a long way from Barbados that, going to his home for a good West Indian meal, I met him and no regrets ... there was not a lot of West Indian folks around at that time, so when you did get to meet one it was great.

Well, Bristol has changed a great deal over nearly forty years since I was living here. All I can say is if you can live in Bristol you can live anywhere.

Esther Phillips was born in a small village, Breton, in St Philip's in Barbados. She came to England in 1956 to take up nursing training as a result of the major campaign to recruit people from the West Indies after the war. She has retired from Southmead Maternity Hospital after 31 years. She has four daughters and two grandchildren. On their 40th wedding anniversary, Esther and her husband went on a Caribbean cruise. She is an active member of the Barbados Parents and Family Association.

OLIVE LACK

Think Fondly of England

I was nursing in St Lucia in the West Indies for six years. I had then gone back to my home in Antigua for two years, and I wanted to do some more studies. Mainly I wanted to do opthalmic nursing and the only way I could do so satisfactorily was to come out to study -- and I knew I could study ... I had done that already.

I had no fear whatsoever of coming to England on my own. In those days, I thought I could do everything on my own! I was in my early thirties and it was September, 1961. I came by boat as I couldn't afford to come by plane. It was a harrowing experience! I am not a good sailor -- I am afraid of the sea, and I didn't know I could be so sea-sick! I was sea-sick for the whole of the journey -- nearly two weeks. You do make friends on the boat, they were all people from the Caribbean and for me it wasn't a problem. I just didn't like feeling sea-sick. When in England, I kept in touch with one or two of the people from the boat until I got lost in what I had to do, I had no time to look back ...

I went to work in Mount Vernon Hospital in Northwood, Middlesex. I thought I was going to do a shortened course in general nursing. I though I had arranged it beforehand, and then I would go on to do ophthalmic nursing as part of a post-graduate course. I had to sit in Mount Vernon for three years and go through all the general nursing training again. But if you want something badly enough, you do it ...

The General Nursing Council wrote to say they thought of Antigua as just a cottage hospital and they couldn't give me a reduction. That was right at the end, and the three years had nearly ended anyway, so I just said put it down to experience and get on with the business of living!

At first, I had nobody at all here that I knew. Again, if you want to do something badly enough, you do it. You lived in the nurses' home and you were sheltered. There was a cafeteria, you could have all your meals there. You travelled if you wanted to, because you were salaried. So life wasn't difficult for me, I made friends and we moved around together. But studying ... I loved to study, and I always enjoyed nursing, but it wasn't my first choice. I had wanted to teach in schools, but I took up nursing and nursing has served me well, and I hope I served it just as well -- no complaints.

I came to Bristol through a friend of my sister, I first came on holiday and it went on from there. I came to Southmead Hospital and went into midwifery.

Before I came to England I knew it would be cold and then it was September, and even though it was supposed to be an Indian summer, I was cold! I lived in the British Council hostel in London for just a few weeks where I made friends, and they were very kind people. Then I moved to the hospital. You went to work, and you went home and you slept and you ate, and you went out if you wanted to with or without your friends. I didn't mind moving about on my own.

What of my impression of the people, especially the nurses I worked with? They were from all over the world, I didn't stop to notice the difference. Differences in race never bothered me. I think it has bothered me as time has gone on, but in those early days -- no, I made friends with just about everybody and I got on with everybody. I got along with senior staff and new staff, I didn't care who they were, I just accepted them for what they were. That was the way I was brought up. People were people, and there were nice people and not-so-nice

people, and you liked someone or you didn't. I didn't have enemies. The differences in nationality never, ever bothered me in those early days.

But over the years you cannot but be aware that people think differently about different people, we just have different values, different expectations, different perceptions of people ... in those early days people were just there, and I was there to do one thing -- to get on with my studies, to get on and to get back home to Antigua -- oh yes, that was on the cards very much, I wanted to go back ...

But I didn't. I got married. Don't ask me about my marriage. It was lovely, and now it's ended and I am going back to Antigua. I hope I can give to Antigua some of what I have ... I am sure that if my health lasts I will be able to find some place, some means of contributing. We haven't got all the expertise in Antigua that you've got here. All the islands could do with as much help as they can get. Alright, they are poor, they may not pay and expect me to do some voluntary work, but if you feel like doing voluntary work, there is a place for you. If you want a salary, are you thinking only of the money or the contribution you can give?

I think I have much to give, I intend to. I decided to go back after my husband died and I was alone. You can't be alone. And, having a big question mark over my health, logic dictates that I go home to be with family. I have retained my friendship with the people I grew up with, because over time I went home every two or three years. When my parents were alive that was important to me, and then after they died I still went back. I was at home last year.

I feel British and I feel Antiguan and I think it's very natural that you are going to feel akin to the people and the place you have spent a large part of your early life, where your brothers and sisters are -- you are still a part of them. You have imbibed so much of the British way of life that you are also British -- but then, you're not British. Will I

be seen as a foreigner when I go back? I've been going back over the years, mixing with my brothers and sisters, we're always on the telephone every weekend. I'm not cut off, I don't feel strange, and if I go back to live I have them around anyway ... it will take a fair amount of adjusting, because I will be over there all the time -- all the shopping, the paying of bills is done differently, but I keep saying -- what others have done, I'm sure I can do -- I know I can do it, I can adjust.

My parents were philosophical about my leaving Antigua. They knew what I aimed at -- getting further studies and more experience in nursing -- and if it was anything that will push you forward, my parents were for it. Parents don't like you to leave home but they know what it's all about, yes. Don't ask me about the size of my family! It is large! But there were brothers and sisters doing the same thing as I've done. Some have gone back, or near enough to Antigua, and they've made their contribution to Antigua. Those who were left are still working quite happily there, and the community know they are there, contributing in their own way.

It makes quite an impact on people's lives when they have to leave their children behind with the grandparents bringing them up, hoping and planning for the day when they can send for them. Sometimes those children become adults not with their parents but with their grandparents, and the backlash is that they do not acknowledge or respect their parents. Their parents have been disappointed when their children do come over and there can be a rift -- it is almost inevitable that there won't be harmony.

The children will say, 'you didn't bring me up, so don't correct me. My grandmother taught me to do it this way ...' I never experienced this, because I never had any children, but my parents gave me their blessings to come to England ...

When I first came here, I hardly ate. It wasn't so much that I missed the food from the West Indies but I didn't like the salads on a winter's night, I didn't like the pork pies and cold meats. I preferred hot dinners. But I had a problem with food anyway -- from childhood to today, food does not come at the top of my priorities -- I eat only to live. I don't fuss about food. I run a home and anyone who comes will not starve, and I can prepare it, but food is for nutrition and often I just forget to eat.

I did not go out searching for West Indian food. I know where to find yams and potatoes and bananas and all sorts in Bristol, but I can never find the sweet potatoes that I really like, because I don't know how to test them in the shop before I buy! I've given up looking for my favourite sweet potato. If friends find good ones, they share them. How on earth do they know the difference?

Bristol was not like London. It was a slow pace, a nice, easy pace. I could find my way around and team up with friends. But even though Londoners are too busy to notice you very much, if you wanted to talk to someone, they would quite happily talk to you. When I came here, to Bristol, I wasn't able to talk to anybody! It's a funny thing, but in Bristol you don't feel as free to talk to people as you did in London ... and this has filtered down to young people and to West Indian children. They don't open up to you very easily, they do so to their peers, they open up to their families, but not to others. They don't seem to be like we used to be back home, not that you should expect them to be anyway, and you don't intrude.

Quite a number of the young people want to go back to the Caribbean to work. They feel they will be happier there working. I don't know what their expectations are, but if they are prepared to give what they can, and get paid for it, if they are prepared to work hard at what they have chosen to do, if they are prepared to recognise that they are not British, and not bringing their British ways to the Caribbean just to change things, they'll be alright. They are going back for ease, not so much peace of mind, but to feel comfortable. The job situation here in Britain for West Indians is not as pleasant as they would like it to be.

Did I have any ideas of what England was going to be like before I came here -- having gone through the school system? Shall I describe it? England was Solid, Sane, Sensible -- as Sensible as the clothes marked 'Made in England'! The English character was basically Decent, Honest, None to Beat ... anything that was British was sound ... no twists or turns ... America was gangsters and of course for money making, but when it came to Decency and Order and Soundness, the British character in those days -- you couldn't beat it. This is how we looked up to Britain. When I got here, that didn't alter immediately. It altered with time and experience ... yes, it altered with time and experience ... but, do you know, even now if you get a dress or any other garment and it's marked 'Made in England', the finish is usually better. But maybe it's me hanging on to a dream, you know?

I served the nursing profession, and it served me well. Leave it at that. It fulfilled something in my life. I had a good marriage. I don't ask much more of Life. I did what I wanted to do ... I did it to the best of my ability. And now it's over. It's a chapter closed ...

What's the first thing I am looking forward to when I get back to Antigua? Not doing anything! Taking in some sunshine and looking around to see where I can fit in, what the needs of the island are. I have to decide my priorities, because the needs are many, and you're not getting any younger. You have to do something that you can manage.

I feel sad now that I am packing ... you cannot spend 36 years in a country with friends and home life and not feel sad to be giving it all up. There is nothing driving me out except logic. Memories are there ... the bad ones -- I'm not taking them with me, I'm going to leave them at Heathrow Airport -- and I'm going to take the good ones with me. I will always think fondly of England. I always will.

"I came to England when I was younger. I don't remember feeling different or strange, but I wondered why a lot of people were going grey or losing their hair colour at an early age. I didn't know then that people had hair colour that wasn't black."

Teacher who came as a child from Bengal

Books published by **New Words**

New Words

The Origins Project has grown out of the New Words community publishing initiative which has so far published three books on topics of popular interest or concern.

Suspended Sentences

Crime, or the fear of crime, is something that touches us all.   Most people have strong feelings about the rising crime rate, and what should be done about it. But they rarely have the chance to have their say.   Suspended Sentences gives that chance, with 30 contributions, a mix of true-life stories, opinions, fiction and poetry.

ISBN 1 872971 64 4   210mm x 150mm   93 pages. £4.99

Dream On

From dream palace to multiplex -- the flicks ... talkies ... the pictures ... films ... the movies.   Whatever we've called it down the years, cinema's played a big part in all our lives. More than 50 local people spell out what cinema means to them.

ISBN 1 872971 68 7   230mm x 210mm   96 pages, with many illustrations. £6.50

Football Crazy

60 fans, of all ages, have their say in this unique book, celebrating the agony and the ecstasy, the power and the glory -- and the sheer craziness of being a football fan.   Women fans have their say, whether puzzling over football's own arcane language, or admitting to an obsession just as strong as the men's.   There are 'think' pieces, too, about football violence, the game's psychology, and the part superstition plays in changing a team's fortunes.

ISBN 1 872971 54 7   230mm x 210mm   96 pages, with many illustrations. £5.99

These titles can be purchased from local bookshops or direct from Redcliffe Press Ltd, 81g, Pembroke Road, Bristol BS8 3EA, adding £1 carriage for one book or £2 for two books or more.